Emma Ayres is a graduate of the Royal Northern College of Music, where she won prizes for chamber music and viola, the Royal Academy of Music and the Hochschule der Künste in Berlin. She has studied with members of the Amadeus Quartet, William Pleeth, Simon Rowland-Jones and Bruno Giuranna.

After playing the viola professionally for ten years, Emma began her radio career in 2001. She worked initially at Radio Television Hong Kong, and after immigrating to Australia in 2003 joined ABC Classic FM. She still plays her viola, and has recently played with the Bombay Chamber Orchestra and the Afghan Youth Orchestra, about which she has made two radio documentaries.

You can follow Emma on Twitter @emmaayresviola

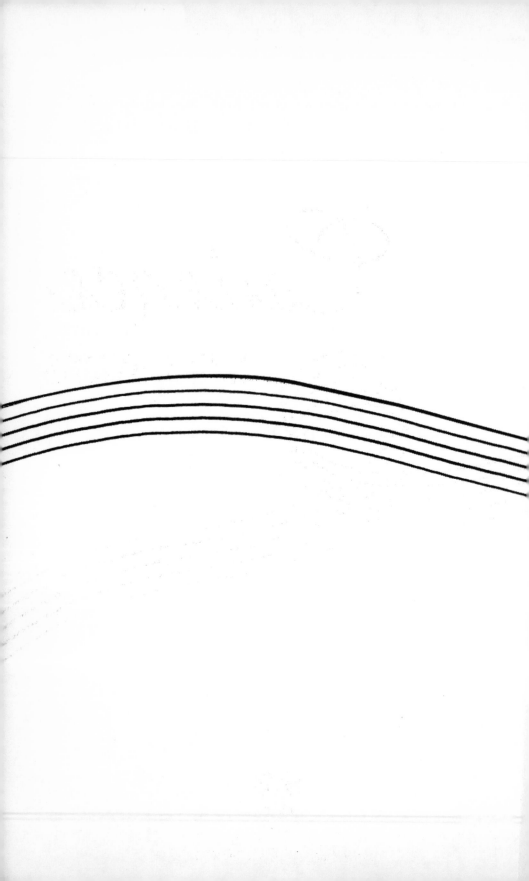

Cadence

EMMA AYRES

ABC
Books

The ABC 'Wave' device is a trademark of the
Australian Broadcasting Corporation and is used
under licence by HarperCollins*Publishers* Australia.

First published in Australia in 2014
by HarperCollins*Publishers* Australia Pty Limited
ABN 36 009 913 517
harpercollins.com.au

HarperCollins*Publishers*
Level 13, 201 Elizabeth Street, Sydney NSW 2000, Australia
Unit D1, 63 Apollo Drive, Rosedale, Auckland 0632, New Zealand
A53, Sector 57, Noida, UP, India
77–85 Fulham Palace Road, London W6 8JB, United Kingdom
2 Bloor Street East, 20th floor, Toronto, Ontario M4W 1A8, Canada
10 East 53rd Street, New York NY 10022, USA

Ayres, Emma, author.
  Cadence / Emma Ayres.
  ISBN: 978 0 7333 3189 3 (paperback)
  ISBN: 978 1 7430 9866 0 (ebook)
  Ayres, Emma – Travels.
  Women broadcasters – Australia – Biography.
  Women musicians – Australia – Biography.
  Other Authors/Contributors:
  Australian Broadcasting Corporation.
791.44092

Cover design and illustration by Hazel Lam, HarperCollins Design Studio
Front cover image by Lisa Tomasetti
Back cover images supplied by Emma Ayres
Photo frame images by shuttesrtock.com
Typeset in 10/15pt ITC Bookman by Kirby Jones
Printed and bound in Australia by Griffin Press
The papers used by HarperCollins in the manufacture of this book are a natural,
recyclable product made from wood grown in sustainable plantation forests. The fibre
source and manufacturing processes meet recognised international environmental
standards, and carry certification.

5 4 3 2 1   14 15 16 17

For my mother, who made me
and for Jane, who makes me who I am

'It's never too late to have a happy childhood'

– Tom Robbins

C major/minor

When I was eight years old, my mother asked me the most important question of my life.

'Emma, what instrument do you want to play?'

A simple question: what sounds do you like? What do your friends play? Who is your favourite music teacher at school? Do you, in fact, particularly care what instrument you play? Or will it simply be a way of passing the time until you find something else to distract you?

Or a question of great depth and difficulty, one that you may not ever be able to answer, a koan; you may as well ask, what language would you like to speak for the rest of your life? What type of people will your friends be? What will evolve to be your fundamental philosophical tenets? Who, indeed, do you want to *be* in this world?

Seeing as I was only eight, I thought the question was the former.

'I want to play the cello.'

My mum put me down for the violin.

I hated the violin. My second sister Penny played it and my mum Anne had played it until she was sixteen, when she sold her instrument to buy make-up; the two of them fought bitterly over how long Penny should practise and in my child's mind the violin and the shrillness it brought were hideous.

Most importantly, the violin was not the cello. Jacqueline du Pré played the cello, Mr Fairbanks, the cool teacher at school with the corduroy trousers and the big beard, played the cello; I wanted to join them and play the cello too, I wanted to be the source of its sound. My desired instrument ended up in the hands of my older brother Tim. He gave up after a year.

In England in the late seventies there was a network of peripatetic music teachers who travelled around in each county teaching groups and individuals, all for free. Then, when you could read music and had maybe passed a couple of exams, you could go along and play with the youth orchestra of your standard and start to swim in the universe of music and musicians.

My first violin teacher was Mrs Llewellyn. Every week at school she taught three of us children together, for half an hour. If my own gatekeeper was anything to go by, this musical universe was an eccentric place indeed; Mrs Llewellyn was an extremely tall woman, in her sixties and already bowed with scoliosis, draped with numerous shawls and hair fraying from her thinning bun. I would later go to her home for lessons where she kept a silent husband, a cat called Yorick and a spotty son who played the organ. She was mostly kind, suddenly mean and in that first lesson taught us how to read the notes in manuscript for the four open strings of the violin. G, down the bottom with two extra lines because it is SO low; D, hanging out underneath the stave for shelter; A, all relaxed in the middle and looking up to E, perched on top and very, very screechy. E for screechy.

Afterwards I walked home proudly across the fields with my own violin; well, it belonged to the school, but I didn't care. I also didn't care about the cardboard case, which was falling apart, and the crude instrument and bow, which had been made by Mr and Mrs Skylark in China. And at the time I didn't care that it was not a cello. All I knew was that I had a friend forever.

It was a Friday, which meant Gran'ma would be coming round for dinner. We had fish on Fridays. Casserole on Saturdays, roast something on Sundays, cold roast on Mondays, mince on Tuesdays, sausages on Wednesdays (those two could be swapped), liver on Thursdays and fish on Fridays. Gran'ma came for the fish and the roast. The six of us in our permanently allotted chairs ate dinner silently and afterwards I showed Gran'ma my violin.

'Can I play you something, Gran'ma?'

'No, you can't play anything. You haven't learnt to play anything yet.'

My mother's brutal reminder had nothing to do with grammar. My first performance and my enthusiasm were shattered before I could even begin. I put my violin back in its case to wait for a time when I *could* play something.

Perhaps this is a good point at which to state quite bluntly that my childhood was desperately unhappy. I was that child who sat at the edge of the group. Fat, frowning, silent, uncertain and, most important to other children, unhappy-looking. And therefore picked on.

So the fat: well, puppy fat, never mind. But the frowning, that came from an early need to try to work out where happiness lay. It didn't visit us at home very much. There was the small issue of my parents' divorce when I was two, after which Anne had had a nervous breakdown and John Ernest George had married the next-door neighbour and moved to Singapore. In the space of two years Mum had gone from being a married, privileged expatriate living in Nigeria, with servants, games of bridge and drunken curry lunches, to working part time as a civil servant and looking after four children (with only four and a half years between us) in the middle of England in a small, dull town. Happiness doesn't have much room to manoeuvre in such conditions. There was a lot to frown about.

The silence was simply a survival mechanism. What does an animal do when all around is doubt, insecurity and risk? It keeps a low profile. My poor mother had the most desperate moods, as she tried to bring us up with only her parents' help, very little money, no friends and an enormous, rejected love that would not sit down and surrender. Dad came and visited once a year, for a day. For appearances. That eventually drifted off to maybe once every few years. But still, he was the *man*, he was the cool guy with loads of money, presents, a car (we never had one) and a day of fun. He never sent birthday or Christmas cards on time, but isn't it extraordinary how full of faith a child can be? My birthday is in February and every morning I would hope that a card might be shoved through the letterbox with one of those exotic Singaporean stamps on it. I'd wait until about November, and then start to look forward to Christmas instead. I didn't give that up until I was thirty, when my brother Tim told me that Dad said he couldn't be bothered to call on my birthday. Twenty-eight years. I gave it a good go.

I eventually worked out that if Mum were in a good mood in the morning, she certainly wouldn't be by the evening. In her wretchedness to try to keep things together, we had an order for everything. In the morning we would get up, stand in a line at the top of the stairs and go down, still in line, and have a hot drink. Then, as we took it in turns to wash or be washed, the others would make beds and get dressed. Then we would line up again — Liz, Penny, Tim and me — in order of age, to have our hair brushed. Breakfast was cooked, always (no tatty cardboard food in our house), and then we walked over the playing fields and railway line to school. We were the only children we knew who came from a so-called broken home. Our home wasn't broken, it was crushed. Crushed by everybody in it wanting to be somewhere or someone else.

When I introduce a child to their cello or viola or violin, I make a point of two things: one, I teach them a little open string plucking piece they can play to their grandmother when they get home, and two, I make sure they understand that this new thing they have in their life can transform them; it really can be their best friend; it will always be there for them when their thighs are fat, their chin has the world's largest zit on it and their period has come unexpectedly in gym when they have to wear a leotard (btw isn't that the cruellest garment?). An instrument in a child's life, anybody's life, is an avatar of hope, of change and improvement, of communication with others, but perhaps most importantly with your self.

So even though I didn't want to play the violin, after my first lesson I knew I had found a way out of my horrible life. I now had a reason to be alone, which was a big deal as I shared a bedroom with Liz and Penny and the only time I had on my own was on the loo. Who would willingly be in the same room as a beginner violinist? And who interrupts someone when they're practising? I had a way of releasing all that melancholy that my

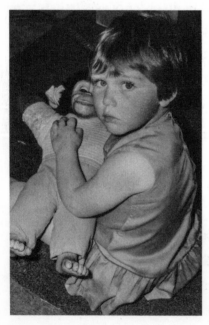

A very worried-looking five-year-old. I was allowed to take my favourite gorilla home from play school for the weekend.

mind absorbed through the day. I had something that wasn't going to disappear overseas then only show up once a year; I had something that didn't have mood swings. In fact, I had a relationship at my fingertips, which continues to this day.

I played with the Hong Kong Philharmonic Orchestra for nearly eight years.

I joined the orchestra at the beginning of 1992, after auditioning in a dank, gas-smelling room up the Finchley Road in North London. I didn't think I had a hope. There were so few jobs for violists at the time and this one was particularly attractive: good salary (any salary was good), long holidays and let us not forget the location and the moment: 1992 and Hong Kong, coming up to one of the strangest terminations of a contract that the world had ever seen. In 1898 the British Government had signed a ninety-nine year lease to extend their land in Hong Kong and that lease was due to end on 30 June 1997. Margaret Thatcher realised that there was not much chance of Deng Xiaoping signing a new contract, so in a few years' time there was going to be an epoch-making event that would affect millions of people; I had a chance to witness this, perhaps even have a tiny part, if I could only play my orchestral excerpts in tune and in time.

Orchestral auditions are savage things. They can be so cursory. The applicant has (usually) been playing their instrument for twenty or so years. They have continued playing when many of their friends have given up, mostly at the beginning of puberty.

They have practised slow, long notes for sound and intonation, often in the form of scales and arpeggios, hundreds of thousands of times. They have worked obsessively with a metronome to develop speed and NASA-precise coordination. They have developed the sensitivity of their hearing to the point where the slightest change in pitch is like a boulder on the freeway. They have got up at 5.30am to squeeze in practice before school; they have missed out on weekends as they stay in to prepare for a concert; they have been taught by teachers who themselves are descended from some of the greatest musicians in our history (I can claim Beethoven as my great- great- great- great- great- grand teacher, and you know what? I choose to do so). They have committed to memory hours of the most complicated and beautiful music mankind has created. These people are highly trained musical Olympians, the difference from sporting Olympians being that they have to pay their own university fees. The similarity being, one minuscule error and you are out of the running.

It was a devastatingly dark and wet day in November, the sort Philip Larkin writes so perfectly about, when I travelled to London from the Midlands for my audition. I would not have much time to warm up when I got to the audition place, even in the unlikely event the train was on time, so I practised in the train toilets between Birmingham and Milton Keynes. Strauss' *Don Juan* opening riff would either comfort people's distressed bladders or provoke them into calling the guard.

Someone called the guard.

'You can't play in the train toilet.'

The fact is, I could, and was actually rather proud of the fact. Do you realise how difficult it is to practise in a British rail loo? There are many technical issues to deliberate over. Sit or stand? Angle your bow over the water swilling in the loo or over the water swilling in the sink? If it all goes horribly wrong, what do you write on the insurance claim? Where do you put your case, and most tricky of all, where do you balance your music? All of this had been brilliantly negotiated; I had swashbuckled my way through *Don Juan* and was just getting tucked into the scherzo from Mendelssohn's *Midsummer Night's Dream*, dreaming of a job in the sun and enough money to buy a better instrument.

'Can't play in the train toilet'? I don't think so.

I returned to my seat. Lucky I'd been practising for sixteen years beforehand.

I stepped into the audition room, in my favourite (not) Laura Ashley dress. Not only was I in a situation that was unnatural and fraught, I was wearing clothes that made me feel unnatural and fraught. A dress on an androgynous lesbian never works.

For auditions there is generally a set piece or pieces, either solo or with piano, to show off certain musical and technical abilities (or lack thereof), then a set of orchestral excerpts, which do the same. I played solo Bach first, the Prelude to the D Minor Suite. This was not a particularly shrewd choice; the prelude is not very challenging technically, although it does show your sense of phrasing and rubato.

Rubato is, or at least should be, a very subtle skill. It means 'to rob' in Italian and the idea is that the main beats of the bar stay in the same place, but by 'robbing' from one, that is, taking a little more time, you pay back in the next beat or so. William Pleeth, Jacqueline du Pré's teacher, described it to my quartet as the beats being like a picture frame, which stays firm, and the picture moves around inside. Rubato is not necessarily high on the list of requirements if you are applying for a job in a section. Section players, those sitting behind the first two in a string section, are called the rank and file and they do what they are told; rank and file is the official term, but some people like to call it wank and smile. And they often do.

Rubato thoroughly shown off, I was then asked to play the opening flourish of Richard Strauss' *Don Juan*. This is a regular requirement for string auditions and it demonstrates the ability to do the musical version of bullshitting. An American orchestra once practised this piece for weeks in anticipation of Strauss coming to conduct them; in the first rehearsal he stood on the podium, waved his enormous baton and off the strings went with the opening breakneck statement. Strauss crashed his baton down on the music stand in front of him and said, 'No, no, no!' (It may well have been nein, nein, nein.) 'I don't want to hear all the notes!'

So the idea is to play all the notes, but for it not to seem like you played all the notes. Sort of like Magritte meets Jackson Pollock. I took a couple of directions from David Atherton, who was the music director of the orchestra at that time, then was asked to play the Mendelssohn Scherzo. The scherzo demands quite the opposite in skills to the Strauss; you need to be perfectly poised, your bow dropping down onto the string about ten times per second, each drop exactly at the same moment one of your left-hand fingers has prepared the note; actually the left hand needs to be fractionally early. One hiccup and you fall over. Although not usually literally.

So that was it. After all those years, all those lessons, all those concerts and all those choices to stay and practise, not do something else, my audition was finished.

'So, Miss Ayres, when can you move to Hong Kong?'

'Darling, don't forget to use talc between your thighs!'

From the day I left on the Cathay Pacific 747 to fly thirteen hours to Hong Kong with my mother's final words of advice ringing in my ears and me ruing the lack of talc in my luggage, to the day I left the stage of the Hong Kong Cultural Centre for the final time, I had grown up. I had fallen in love, I had taught at a Vietnamese Detention Centre, I had played hundreds of concerts with famous musicians, I had travelled extensively around Asia, but in my heart I knew I had not done as much as I could. For the latter part of my time there I felt I had allowed my life to become shallow and superficial. I was being paid to do what I loved, but people who no longer loved playing surrounded me. I knew that if I stayed in the orchestra my life would become stagnant.

We fight and struggle to get to a certain position, but, usually in a brilliant and devastating moment, we realise that *that* place is no longer where we want to be. We need to be somewhere else. Simply, we have stopped growing. Looking around at some of the older members of the band, I saw two choices. Either you stopped caring about your art and kept smiling, or you stopped caring about your art and frowned. Plants need to be repotted when they become root-bound and so do we.

The day I decided I needed to leave was a sort of musical perfect storm: the orchestra was in the theatre pit playing ballet music, slowly enough that the dancers could fit in their steps and not fall flat on their faces, but so slowly that the music *did* fall flat on its face; there was some particularly uninspiring, bullying conducting and some of my colleagues were playing video games, reading books and missing their cues. I looked around the darkened pit, smelled the lackadaisical attitude and wrote my resignation letter that night. I had NO idea what I was going to do, no idea where I would live, no idea whether I would keep on playing the viola, no idea whether I would even keep on living in a musical universe. I just knew that if I stayed in that orchestra, I would not be living the life I had wanted as a child. All that wonder of my eleven-year-old self, cycling through the lanes of Shropshire, would wither into unfulfilment and eventually illness. I didn't want to know where the road ended before I had got there and if I stayed in Hong Kong I could see exactly where it would end – depression and alcoholism.

By writing that resignation letter I was sending myself into the void. If I weren't a musician, who would I be?

I suppose it is fairly unusual to decide at the age of thirty-one that you want to cycle across Europe and Asia, but why go from England to Hong Kong? Why not cycle through Africa, or the length of the Americas?

Chris, a mate in New York, came to visit Hong Kong. We went cycling up in the north in the New Territories, which had now been handed back to China along with the rest of the colony. Making idle chat is common with friends; you have probably made some idle comment today even, but be warned! Those idle comments, they can have enormous, life-changing consequences.

As we ambled along on our bicycles I idly uttered seven words, seven words that would change the course of my life.

'You could cycle from here to Paris.'

You know when you say something quite casual and then at some point the casualness falls away and you realise the significance of the statement? A small remark looked at attentively can often touch your quick more than the lengthiest statement.

There was a hiatus. Chris looked at me puzzled (geography clearly not his strong suit) and questioned the feasibility of this observation. Over that weekend we tried to draw a world map, with laughable results. Mediaeval cartographers did so much better, however I did manage to prove to Chris (and reassure myself) that you could cycle to Paris from Hong Kong and that there were only borders, and no seas, in the way. After I had done my bit for American education, the casualness of the remark started to fall away. Over the next few weeks I cycled round Hong Kong Island on my daily ride, negotiating the six million inhabitants and wondering what I was going to do with the rest of my life, but the thought of this epic trip kept nudging me. Cycling travel books leapt off the shelves of bookshops into my arms and made me read them till late into the night; I would lie in bed thinking about the route I could take. This was it. This was what I should do when I had played out the rest of my contract with the orchestra. I had spent my childhood and teen years inside a small, windowless practice room; I had lived in an internalised world the whole of my life. So yes, I wanted to cycle from England to Hong Kong. What I would do after that would hopefully reveal itself along the way.

During those eight years in Hong Kong I had travelled by aeroplane back and forth to England at least once, sometimes twice, a year. Between naps, films and gin and tonics I had often lifted the window shade, looking down to the earth ten thousand metres below and fantasising about what was going on down there. As turbulence rocked the plane as we crossed the Himalayas, what lives were people pursuing in the mountains? What does a yak smell like? How does a marmot sound? When did you know for sure you were in the Himalayas, or merely the foothills, or on the plains? What were those bright lights in the desert as we crossed Iran? Did anybody travel in Kazakhstan when it looked completely white and frozen deep from above? What were people eating for breakfast in Turkey? Does Turkish bread taste better there? And most importantly, how did all these places flow from one to another? Was there a clear change from one side of the border to the other, or was there a gradual, almost imperceptible metamorphosis of landscape, culture and sentiment? I wanted to know and I wanted to feel the distance. Cycling, you might agree, would certainly allow me to do that.

I studied maps to work out the ideal route; I researched visa details, including how long a visa lasted and whether that included the time from when it was issued (definitely a cyclist's problem); I read bicycle magazines and pored over tyre choices and the different benefits of an aluminium- or a steel-framed bicycle. And I came to the conclusion that it was just going to be too hard. I decided not to do it.

Alexander the Great changed my mind. Actually it was a TV program with Michael Wood about Alexander the Great: where he had managed to travel, the obstacles he had overcome, the gaps in mountains he had filled with logs to get his army through and the adventures he had had in such strange new worlds. And all I was put off by was a bit of paperwork. Alexander changed my mind, but perhaps even more so than him, my ninety-year-old self changed my mind. If you are not sure whether or not you should do something, ask your ninety-year-old self. (If you are ninety, um, ask your thirty-one-year-old self?) My older self replied that now, in my early thirties, with enough youth to cycle that far and maybe just enough age to make sensible decisions, with enough money in the bank to do it but not so much that I would be lazy, now was the right time. And I would regret it if I didn't. And the mere threat of regret is a VERY powerful thing.

I decided I would do it.

On my own. Yes, I did, do even, have friends, but no friends at that point with time or money to spare and anyway, isn't travel nearly always better alone? At this point my partner Jane leans over, pokes me in the ribs and says something contradictory. Hence the words 'nearly always' …

Travelling alone is obviously a risk in some ways. However, I did, and do still, believe that the advantages are worth it. The greatest benefit by far is that you have only yourself to rely on and you get to know yourself, grubby, weak bits and all. Travel goes inwards as much as outwards. You would be surprised to see Socrates on a package tour (although a good package tour does have a lot of things going for it). Another significant benefit, which became clearer the further I travelled from England, was that when the overwhelmingly huge majority of people see a single woman, they want to make sure she is safe. In many countries this meant inviting me into their family home, cooking me dinner, giving me their bed and lending me their pyjamas. This is far less likely to happen if there are even two of you. Who has two spare sets of pyjamas? The assumption then would be that you looked after one another. That you would have your own pyjamas. Three or more, forget it. Your very presence has already substantially changed the place you have come to see, just like the famous scientific experiment conundrum. And the way I saw some couples talk to each other in slightly stressful circumstances, it clearly doesn't always hold true that fellow travellers look after each other. In travel, veritas. One issue was that many people thought I must be sad and lonely to be obliged to travel on my own, but there was always, in desperate circumstances, the gold ring on my wedding finger and the promise of an imaginary husband waiting at the next big town. If you want to know, his name is Michael, he is a university English professor and he is still waiting at the next town. He may be waiting some time.

You never feel truly alone, anyway, if you have an instrument with you. I decided that I had to have an instrument, but that taking my viola would perhaps be a little too heavy both in a physical and a metaphorical way. And playing along the way would give me a new perspective on the possibilities of music. So I borrowed a very cheap and cheerful three-quarter length violin (gasp) from one of my students and there she sat on my back, Aurelia, named after the Roman road round the coast north of Pisa, in her supremely light cardboard case, for sixteen thousand kilometres. A kilogram of joy and a giver of hundreds of evenings of entertainment, endless companionship and not a bad topic for discussion.

For such an enormous physical journey, I felt like I needed a musical journey to match. Bach wrote six suites for solo cello and six sonatas and partitas for solo violin. He was a relatively young man when he wrote them, working for the Prince of Anhalt-Cöthen; his first wife Maria Barbara was still alive when he wrote the violin pieces and they only had seven children (Bach went on to have twenty); the responsibilities of his job in Leipzig and his church gig were yet to wear Johann down and he delighted, clearly, in writing this secular, deceptively simple music. Viola players play all the suites, sonatas and partitas, one of the splendid benefits of the instrument. They are an enormous technical challenge, though, particularly the violin sonatas, and I had only got to grips with a small amount of this music in six years of music college. So I photocopied the sheet music, reduced it to a slightly smaller size than this book and, hey presto, I had myself a travelling show. At least, a challenge.

That's the beauty of playing an instrument — you can always go further. Just like cycling.

* * *

The third cello suite by Bach, particularly the two bourrées in C major then C minor, is a terrific piece for playing in impromptu settings. Well, a bourrée *is* a drinking song.

Actually, I've just realised that across several Muslim countries I entertained people by playing them a drinking song. Oops. Sorry!

Sometimes, a bourrée can be just the ticket. I was just leaving Pakistan, about to go over one of the most hotly contested borders in the world. I had had my British passport stamped by a ridiculously smartly dressed Immigration officer, all the time feeling guilty because: a) I was born in the country that caused the whole mess in the first place, and b) doesn't everyone feel guilty at Immigration? Or is that just me? I left the office and, as instructed, walked my bike (under no circumstances are you allowed to cycle your bike) towards the gate into enemy territory, a.k.a. India.

I had left Lahore, in Pakistan, very early in the morning to get to the India–Pakistan border by 9am and to try to arrive in Amritsar, in India, before I wilted from cycling in forty-five degree heat. Just forty kilometres separate these two cities. Not even the distance of a marathon. Before Partition, people used to go and pay visits to friends and family in the other town and be back in time for tiffin. During Partition, whole trainloads of people were hacked to death, trying to travel to their newly appointed country. When the carriage doors were opened, in both Lahore and Amritsar railway stations, blood poured out in a thick, deep stream.

And now, after Partition, the border is a confusing mixture of supreme distrust, envy and showing-off. Each evening the two defence forces have a flag-lowering ceremony where they try to outdo the other in pomposity and military snappiness.

So you can understand that I was a little nervous walking between the two countries. I didn't look very snappy smart myself. You try looking half-decent with only two shirts to choose from and your whole world stuffed into four panniers. I had washed my cycling kameez particularly thoroughly, though, along with a loving wash of my bicycle, Vita. Passport in hand, I walked the last few metres of Pakistan, a country that I had fallen in love with during its build-up to the monsoon. I was feeling quite disconsolate actually and slightly dragged my feet as I thought of all the kind, hilarious people I had met and wondered if I would ever see them again. I was also a bit nervous, anticipating this new country, India, and what she might bring. I was quite lost in my thoughts when abruptly to my right a ranger, one of the border protection special forces of the Pakistani military, shouted out for me to stop. So I did. I stood perfectly still, shitting myself, as this very tall, outrageously handsome, mustachioed sergeant ran up to me and examined my bicycle, my luggage, me and, finally, my violin.

He tapped the case on my back. I had long ago stopped noticing the weight of it so sometimes forgot it was even there. The ranger wanted me to play him something. I knew that because he made the international gesture for, 'Play me something!' which goes like this: you point, or indeed hit the case of the instrument you want to hear; you then look straight into the eyes of the musician and raise both your shoulders and hands in a shrug and a gesture, not unlike Herbert von Karajan in front of the Berlin Philharmonic Orchestra to get them started on a Beethoven symphony.

'Play me something and it had better be good, otherwise I am going to revoke your visa and make your life hell, even though you have officially left the country.'

That's what I also interpreted with that international gesture.

I played some Bach.

It's quite hard to play the violin when you feel like you are playing for permission to advance to the next country. Sort of like a perverse TV show where the contestants are confined in countries far from home, one by one, if they fail to perform well. Or a board game in a Christmas from hell. In fact, it was more nerve-wracking than auditioning for the orchestra all those years ago. At least I had comfortable clothes on this time. I chose a piece I knew well, from memory — the C major bourrée. I knew it so well that I didn't have to think about the piece when I was playing it. My fingers, once they started, were like a little pack of Pavlov's dogs; starting with certain notes made the following ones inevitable. As I played the bourrée I kept my eye on the ranger, especially his rifle, and watched as his moustache twitched with glee. I played just the first boisterous bourrée, in the major key, thinking that if I went on to the slightly lost and morose minor one my new friend would get a little morose himself and then all would be lost. So I stopped, waited for the verdict, and it came.

'Please proceed.'

I had passed Go. Just in time as it turned out, because what looked like his commanding officer was walking over towards us quick march and he didn't look very impressed. He barked an order to the ranger, I packed up my violin as hastily as I could and walked to India.

And, ten minutes away in India, exactly the same thing happened. An Indian soldier this time, making precisely the same international gesture.

This border guard urged me to play the minor bourrée as well, although he started to yawn in the middle and fiddle with my bicycle. I guess my Bach was worse than my bike.

G major/minor

My big sister Elizabeth taught me to ride a bike when I was about six. That seems quite late to start, thinking about it now, but I suppose I was busy. Liz was about ten and she had heavy responsibilities on her beautiful, big shoulders. Mum often used Liz, the eldest, as a sounding board for various issues that were surfacing in our family, most noticeably the problems with Penny. Liz looked after us all and she taught me to ride a bike and to swim. She was my dad.

I learnt on her old blue bike, a Peugeot I think, which she had been given for Christmas when the family was living in Nigeria. Dad ran a factory that repaired rubber-making machinery and he, Mum, Liz and Penny lived for three years in Sapele, on the Benin River. Tim and I spent the very beginning of our lives there, but then we all had to leave at the outbreak of the Biafran

War. Mum travelled home on a refugee ship with the four of us, me a babe in arms, Liz only five, while Dad stayed behind and packed everything up. So Liz's Nigerian blue bike ended up in Shrewsbury with me wobbling on it. It had trainer wheels added, gradually made higher as my wobbles lessened. Until, one sunny Saturday morning, a spring morning just warm enough for me not to have to wear my nylon red anorak, Liz and I went out onto the road in front of our low-slung, mock-Tudor, semi-detached house and a miracle happened. For the first time in my life the combination of my balance and the momentum of the bicycle wheels was perfect. I was cycling. Unassisted, downhill. Which meant I was flying. Or as close as a six-year-old can get. I looked back at Liz, who was waving and cheering, her broad open face in an exultant grin. I promptly crashed into a beech hedge. Looking backwards on a bicycle takes practice.

From then until now, forty or so years later, I have always had a bicycle (I admit that currently I have five; one for every occasion). Until I was eleven I had hand-me-downs, like my clothes, from my siblings. One sibling would have a growth spurt and Mum would reward them with clothes from the next eldest and dump the old clothes in my drawer. Only Liz had regular new clothes, which was understandable. We were poor. As Charles Dickens noted, we were from the most miserable class in English society, the lower-middle class. We had the aspirations of the middle class, but not the money; the lack of money of the working class, but not the pride. So, definitely, no holidays away, no luxuries, no car. Which I see now as a blessing, as it meant that we cycled or walked everywhere.

In Shrewsbury in the seventies the school system was still divided into grammar and secondary modern. In your final year of primary school you took a test, the eleven-plus; depending on your result you either went to the grammar school, boys and girls divided, or the secondary modern. If you went to the secondary modern, you were considered a thickie and a failure. So do the minds of children work. Dad kept his word with only one thing during my childhood — he bought us all a new bike when we passed the eleven-plus. Actually Penny failed it, but she got a bike anyway. Liz, the first to take the test, was bought a navy-blue Raleigh ladies' bike. A step through, with three Sturmey Archer hub gears and moustache handlebars. It was a little too big for her, in the way that first year school uniforms are, anticipating a final size rather than fitting now. She went down to the local bike shop, Mr Jones and Son, to choose the bike with Dad on his yearly visit. He returned to Singapore and his new family and left somebody else to take Liz and her new treadly out for adventures.

Gran'ma came to the rescue. It was the long, boring, six-week summer holiday. Mum had to go to work, so Gran'ma would come to look after us every day; she played Pelmanism with us, did her own version of *Letters and Numbers*, read with us and made us slightly over-cooked poached eggs for lunch. Gran'ma had a car, a golden Hillman Hunter. She, Tressie Doreen, had passed her driving test on the fifth time, when she was fifty-eight. Grandpa had died in a car crash just a few years before and Gran'ma was never a confident driver. But one morning, as she dropped Mum off at work and the four of us were hunching down low in the back seat so she could see out as she reversed, she said that we were going out for a drive and Liz was going to come with her new bike.

Gran'ma understood bicycles and their possibilities. She and Grandpa cycled everywhere together before Mum was born: to the coast in Kent, into London town from Bromley, to work and to weekends. When Mum was old enough, and had come back to live in Bromley after being evacuated to Devon in the Second World War, Gran'ma decided that Anne should learn to ride a bicycle. She could join her parents for those trips that had been interrupted by pesky things like bombs and having children. Anne was put into the stern and capable hands of a PE teacher who lived in the same block. That summer, around the hole in the garden where a V1 rocket had landed, Anne tried to balance on two wheels. She tried to find that miraculous moment, but it never came. My mum never learnt the meaning of 'It's just like riding a bike' from the perspective of actually riding a bike. She and her parents never went on bicycle trips together, and after the war Grandpa bought a car. I always had the feeling from Gran'ma that she mourned those days of cycling and freewheeling in Kent.

So when Gran'ma had the chance to give the gift of cycling to Liz, she took it. We stopped at the baker's to buy a cottage loaf, white with an enormous overweight top, went home to make strange-shaped sandwiches and somehow to get Liz's bike in the boot of the Hillman Hunter. She was stuffed and tied into the boot — the bike that is, not Liz — and off we went down the road into the sublime Shropshire countryside.

If you have never been to Shropshire, may I suggest you do, if at all possible? Shropshire is the largest county in England, with the smallest population; it has the iconic rolling hills of England and the narrow country lanes, it has copses and coppices and streams and larks and meadows and snug little valleys, but it also has a bleak side, with bracken and gorse and rock formations that were named by druids. Shropshire is a place that almost doesn't exist, so fantastic is its nature.

Although Gran'ma was a horribly nervous driver, we loved going around the country lanes with her, especially in summertime. The hedges were so thick and buoyant with leaves that they blocked your view around the corner completely and every time we approached a corner Gran'ma would slow to a near halt and beep her horn. When I drive along country lanes now and do the same thing, a little bit of Tressie nods approvingly. Isn't it reassuring how our grandparents stay with us? Unfortunately Tressie Doreen's driving days didn't last very long. She delivered meals on wheels twice a week, took me with her one day and pulled out in front of a car at a T-intersection. Tressie spent the night in hospital, I have a knobbly scar on my head and I don't think the meals in the boot made it. Gran'ma never drove again.

But that day was perfect. Gran'ma drove out of the town a little to a village called Condover, pulled over and pulled out the bike from the boot. Liz hopped on, the rest of us got back in the car and we drove cautiously past the sycamore, the oak and the sticky beech hedges decorated with blackberry, as Liz rode behind us. The three of us kids knelt on the golden-coloured back seat and watched as Liz pedalled furiously up the hills and then freewheeled down, streamers of delight pouring from her young girl's face. Cycling may have skipped a generation, but boy were we going to make up for it.

I had hand-me-down bikes for a few years and threw myself and them around quite happily. The only restriction from Mum was that we had to be home by late afternoon. Since Mum didn't drive and had never experienced the freedom of freewheeling, she rarely had moments of liberation and deliverance from the almost insurmountable tasks that faced her. There was no way out. Very rarely, maybe once a year, usually late on a Friday afternoon, she would have an overwhelming outburst of despair and walk out. I would watch from the landing window as she walked away from the house and worry frantically that she might not ever come back. She would, eventually, and a kind of equilibrium returned. So these weekends were crucial in the balance of our family life; Mum had her own small pieces of freedom when she chucked us out of the house on a Saturday morning with the instruction, 'Don't come back till tea!' So we didn't. I outgrew the Nigerian blue bike, went on to Liz's next bike and just as that was getting too small the day came for me to take the eleven-plus exam. Tim had passed it the year before, but Penny hadn't. This wasn't at all to say that Penny couldn't, she simply chose not to. Her way in life was not through the confines of a grammar school.

Tim was now in his first year at the local boys' grammar, with his brown, square-framed glasses, his greasy hair and his puppy limbs, which every day wrapped themselves around his new bike, a racer. Ten gears, red, fast. I wanted his bike.

(Actually I did borrow it a few years later to cycle to a hockey tournament. Carrying hockey boots and a hockey stick on the handlebars is never advisable, even less so if the bike is too big for you. I careered down a hill, reached terminal velocity and my hockey boot jammed itself into the front wheel. The bike stopped and I didn't. There was another knobbly scar on my head, a torn shoulder ligament and a delayed viola exam.)

I desperately wanted my own racer. After all, I had put in the work. I had cycled for miles up and down the sharp little hills of Shrewsbury, I had wrestled with one single gear and I had already developed thighs of Tour de France potential. I was ready. My mum, however, was not.

'No, you can't get a racer. They're too fast.'

'Please Mum! I'll be careful!'

'No. You can get a bike like Liz's. A ladies' bike.'

I didn't want a ladies' bike. They were for girls, and I realised at this point that girls just didn't seem to have as much fun as boys. At some dreadful moment in every tomboy's life, we are told that we 'can't behave like that any more' and we are expected to suddenly put on a dress and be lady-like. That moment had occurred already for me about a year earlier, when my brother told me I had to wear a T-shirt and not walk around topless. I hated him for that and envied boys their unfair, physical freedom.

I wore a T-shirt, but there was no way I was getting a ladies' bike. Besides, they only had three gears. When Dad did his annual pull-up in front of the house in a fancy car, Mum told him I couldn't get a racer.

My first bike. The first bike that had not been ridden before by an older sibling, had not been scratched, a bike that had been given only to me. An exquisite, silver Raleigh racer with five gears. A bike that you had to swing your leg over to get on. I was content. Mum was livid. More with Dad of course, than with me. Mum was consistently bad cop, Dad waltzed in, was always good cop and frankly, I don't know how Mum stood it. A lesser woman would have gone mad with grief and frustration.

One problem was that I had no idea how these five-gear, derailleur thingies worked. How did a lever on the down tube of your bike change how hard your pedalling had to be? Once Mum had got used to the idea that her daughter had a racer and not a ladies' bike, she instructed Tim to take me out on a ride and show me how to use the gears. He was not keen. How dorky, having to go for a ride with your kid sister. Tim impatiently explained how the cable pulled the derailleur tight to go to the big cogs, which confusingly were the lower gears, and when you relaxed the cable the derailleur relaxed and guided the chain to the small cogs, which were the thigh-building high gears. Easy. All done with feel, no index gears where your next one is merely a click away. This was art. The art of cycling.

That summer I went mad with glee, hurtling down roads to exotic places like Wig Wig, Longden, Bayston Hill, Meole Brace, Wenlock Edge and Nobold. I took my life savings with me, piles of two pence pieces, huge amounts of money to buy chocolate bars, scones and fizzy drinks to propel me onwards. I felt that I could cycle forever and I did. Cycling, for then and now, was a perfect mixture of security and adventure. The security came from being in charge of my own travel: I propelled myself, I decided where I would go and how quickly or slowly, I decided when I would stop and for how long, and I knew (mostly) how to fix my bicycle. The adventure, well, give a child a bike and you give them the world. But make sure they are back by tea.

When I was twelve, at the end of my first year of grammar school, Robin Thirlby, one of the leading string teachers in the county, told me that I had big hands and that I should play the viola.

My violin playing was not going well. I had flown through the first few grades and loved loved loved my class music teacher at school, Mrs Turner. She was a warm, soft, kind teacher who taught us to read music by taking our hands and writing the notes on the stave on our fingers, and the notes in between the stave on our palms. A brilliant, simple method. When we played the recorder, all we needed to do was stop and check the note and play on. How all thirty of us played together does remain a mystery. Mrs Turner was loved by all, a teacher who influenced thousands of children's lives for the better.

Mrs Llewellyn, on the other hand, was not so inspiring. At this point I was going to her house for lessons, treading softly past her sleeping husband and vicious cat. I played the same three exam pieces over and over and over again for about six months. Then I would take the exam, pass, and go on to three new, slightly harder pieces. I was SO bored. I took to fantasising about Mrs Llewellyn, anything to relieve the torture of that half hour. I felt so guilty because Gran'ma was paying for the lessons, but I wanted to give up the violin.

I scraped through my grade five exam and started to argue with Mum about continuing to play. Everybody else had given up their instruments by this point. Liz had given up the flute, Penny the violin and Tim the cello and the drums. We had had supervised practice every evening, with me going last, of course. Mum had done everything she could to produce a musician; I was the last one standing and there was absolutely no way that Mum was going to concede defeat. And then Robin Thirlby threw me a lifeline — the viola.

I didn't even know what the viola was. Was it a big violin or a small cello? There only ever seemed to be about three viola players in any of the youth orchestras, no matter the size. Viola players seemed elusive, mysterious and in danger of extinction, therefore particularly appealing.

Robin told me that he had a viola I could borrow; I just needed to come up to his house to get it.

Easy, I thought. I can race up, on my racer.

'You can walk,' said Mum. Bikes and new instruments do not mix in the minds of parents.

So I walked. Quite a long way, about six kilometres, and finally arrived at Robin's house. I had never been to a house like his before. Instead of prints of Turner and Constable on the walls like we had at home (on loan from the local library), Robin had violins hanging. He had rugs and colour and vivacity and baroque music decorating his house, not desiccated husbands, like Mrs Llewellyn's.

He handed me a case, significantly larger than my violin case, heavier and deeper, and put a sheath of viola music into my other hand. He explained how the notes were written in different places on the stave, since the viola uses the alto clef, and sent me on my way, with a promise of a lesson the following week.

I walked towards home, desperate to see my new instrument. This first walk together felt like a first date, shy and precious. My (apparently large for my age) hand held the case's handle gently. I adapted my stride so that the viola didn't bang into my leg. I shifted the case from hand to hand, testing which was more comfortable. I glanced down frequently at the case, wondering what delights lay inside and admiring the sturdiness of its shape. Halfway home I couldn't wait any more; I sat down on a bench at a bus stop and put the case on my knee. I opened the latches, lifted the lid, and there she was, my new voice. Bright orange, and proud in her wide, fat frame. She had a label stuck just inside the f-hole that simply said, 'Made in Czechoslovakia'. She had come from a mysterious, hard-to-spell place and I had fallen in love. I closed the case and walked home. I have been playing the viola now for about thirty-five years.

The viola took a while to get used to, after playing the violin for four years. It is longer, wider, deeper and heavier, and the strings are thicker. There is no E string. That meant happiness for other people's ears and mine. No more screeching. The highest string therefore is the A, perched above the alto stave, the D snug in the second space down, the G sitting relaxed on the bottom space and the C string, that particular delight of the instrument, all the way underneath with an extra ledger line. This, the C string, was the sound I was most thrilled by, a chocolate brown, woody, tomboy sound that exhaled compelling, sweet sadness. The bow is slightly shorter and a little heavier; you need to add a bit more arm weight to the bow yourself, especially on the lower strings. The strings are thicker, so you need more finger weight to bring them down onto the fingerboard. Holding the viola itself took quite a while to work out; in fact, I'm still working on it. I eventually got used to the balance of holding it with my head weight on the chin rest, and a little bit of weight taken with the left hand. Once I had become accustomed to these technical things, the musical joys began to reveal themselves. I realised that playing the violin had been like cycling uphill, when I could have been freewheeling down. The violin had been an effort, but in playing the viola I was playing with my heart, so it was effortless.

The first piece of music I fell into completely, body and heart, was the Prelude to the First Cello Suite by Johann Sebastian Bach. Mum was overjoyed with my new ardour for the viola and she would regularly return home with new pieces for me to play. One evening she arrived with a thick edition of the Bach Cello Suites in her hand, the ones I had heard Jacqueline du Pré play. Now I could play them, too; it seemed I didn't need to play the cello after all. I swung the music up onto my spindly music stand and opened the suites at the beginning, the G major one.

When people hear this piece, they often say:

'I wish I could play that. I wish I could play the cello. I wish I hadn't given up when I was twelve/thirteen/hormonal crisis age ...'

Isn't it curious that people never say:

'I am so glad I gave up the [*insert instrument here*]. My life is so much better for not playing it.'

Funny, that.

I looked at the notation of the prelude and it struck me just how beautiful the actual music looked, the notes making wave patterns on the page. It was a chart of a new world, where the tomboy heroine, my viola, got to explore and go on adventures and be brave and scared in equal measure. I launched into the music, soaring and skipping and freewheeling, straining myself in the uphill moments and hurtling down the other side. I played to the end of the piece and went straight back to the beginning; the fun ride got better each time and, after going on this ride thousands of times, it still does.

In the second part of the piece, after a rather dramatic pause, the music goes off into a foreign land of distant(ish) keys and new wave patterns. To bring the piece back to where he started, Bach composed music which takes you on a spectacular journey high up the D string; all you have to do is hold on and swing your bow over to the A string as well. It is music that is actually quite simple to play, but sounds really complicated and, for want of a better word, baroque. The technique is named bariolage and if you ever want to impress your friends and family, this is *it*. It's fancy footwork for string players.

Mum was cooking dinner in the kitchen (Wednesday, therefore sausages) and occasionally she, with a smell of potatoes and onion sauce, came into my room and said,

'That sounds nice, Binx.'

Gran'ma now had something appetising to listen to on Fridays and Sundays.

My career as a musician shifted into a new gear and Mr Thirlby started to teach me. I can't remember the actual handing over of me from one teacher to the other. Perhaps it was something like an Italian mafia movie, done in the shadows of a music room, behind the piano; I do remember that it was slightly scandalous, a sense of a student being poached. I didn't miss Mrs Llewellyn at all, although I did miss Yorick the cat.

Robin was a charismatic teacher: he seduced me into practising, into looking for a better sound and into wanting to be good. No longer was I sent to the back of the second or even third violin section. No, now I was the *viola player*; although I frequently played the same music I had been playing in the third violins, it was now written in the alto clef, therefore special. Suddenly, I was in demand. Violinists were like spare seats at a Schoenberg concert, but viola players were precious property. I was promoted into a higher youth orchestra and had my first moment in the spotlight, proudly barking the sheepdog part in the Spring Concerto from Vivaldi's *Four Seasons*.

It's a very simple part, two identical notes in each bar that essentially go 'woof, woof', the sheepdog insistent as the solo violin sings its shepherd song. However, these were the first two notes in my life that nobody else had, which were mine to shape how I wanted. I took those two notes and put my whole twelve-year-old soul into them. I played like I rode my bike, strongly, determinedly and happily.

On my thirteenth birthday, Mum announced that I should get a paper round. All my siblings had started one at this age, and just because I was the only one who had kept going with my instrument didn't count for anything. Mr Jones (another one, not the bike shop guy; Shrewsbury *is* close to Wales) agreed to take me on at the newsagents. He awarded me the most hated round of them all, one with not many newspapers but a lot of cycling. When I say a lot, thinking back on it now it was probably fewer than ten kilometres, but it seemed like seven leagues at the time. Never mind, though, I had my racer. Every morning Mum came and woke us all up at 6.30am; we put on extra-daggy clothes and cycled down to Mr Jones, collected our papers and went off in different directions. A little elite force of paper children. Except that I was not an A-grade papergirl. I delivered the wrong papers on a fairly regular basis. The big drawback in my paper delivery career, which I think is why I no longer deliver papers, is that I was more interested in what the papers had to say, than who got to read them.

It was a very, very simple task. Each day identical, apart from weekends. You took the paper out of your outrageously heavy paper sack, you checked it had the right address on it, you shoved it in that address's letterbox. Easy. Much harder on the weekend, with the supplements, but still not rocket science. Not easy, however, if you are distracted by fascinating news from South Africa (apartheid), Iran (Iranian Embassy siege) and the Falkland Islands (where?). I pushed a terrifyingly large number of 'Gotcha!' headlines through letterboxes after the *General Belgrano* was sunk.

One morning I was gradually making my way through the Letters to the Editor page between cycling, singing Joni Mitchell's *Blue* (I knew the whole album by heart) and occasionally delivering papers. Music was the distraction in this fairly banal task. Music and the joy of cycling early in the morning. A letter in the Letters' Page caught my eye, one in which Mr Grumpy from Middle England was complaining about paperboys (no mention of papergirls). I put down my sack and opened the paper properly to read on. Mr Grumpy was bemoaning the work ethic of his paperboy and pronounced that the unlikelihood of succeeding in life was already staring these youngsters in the face. If you are doing a bad job at thirteen, you will continue to do so for the rest of your life. I delivered the paper to the wrong house. If only it had been on purpose.

Mr Jones had quite an effect on me about three years later. One morning he asked me if he could show me his penis. I didn't quite understand him, un-strangely enough, and he had to repeat his polite request. I wonder if Mr Grumpy of Middle England ever took these things into consideration, when he bemoaned the uselessness of paper children.

My first experience of chamber music was when I was ten and Mr Fairbanks, he of corduroy trousers, put me in a quartet with Simon

Turner, Kate Harris and a forgettable fourth person. (Why does our child's memory of names always include both the first and the family?) I remember thinking that chamber music was a bit like a sport, but better: you got to play in a team, but there was no opposition and therefore you couldn't lose. We played Boccherini that first time and a few years later I was asked by the big kids to play in a Mozart quintet. The one in G minor with two violas.

Mozart played the viola and so did a whole long, deeply impressive list of other composers — Beethoven, Haydn, Dvorak, Britten, J.S. Bach, Hindemith, Mendelssohn, Hendrix (yes, Jimi) etc. etc. Get the point? Dudes play the viola. Perfectionists play the violin. When Mozart wrote this piece, in 1787, Beethoven was also hanging out in Vienna, hoping to get some lessons from Mozart. There is no evidence of it at all, but I like to think that Mozart and Beethoven sat together as viola players to play through this quintet, the ink barely dry. Mozart chose two violas, not two cellos, for a reason, and surely you would need no more reason than Beethoven?

The quintet is a particularly dark work. When you think about Mozart's music, a lot of the time it is actually quite sunny, isn't it? If it is dark, it really is only as relief from the sunlight in the afternoon, a slight tilting of the Viennese blinds. But in this work, in his Piano Quartet, in his Symphony No. 40 and in the Symphony No. 25, he uses the gloom of G minor to close those blinds completely. They are shut tight in the middle of the day for somebody who doesn't want to go out into the world; no light gets in, in G minor and one of the reasons is that it is the key that resonates most deeply with the violin.

You remember that G-string at the bottom, so low it needs two extra ledger lines? That low G is ever-present in G minor, vibrating in sympathy with the rest of the notes, like a smear of depression. Mozart is thought to have suffered from depression in these latter years, as he was gradually sidelined and had to borrow money from his friends.

The quintet opens with a hasty, unsettling violin tune, with the two violas providing the engine underneath. The violin slips down semitones in despair then looks to the first viola for acknowledgement. The most heart-breaking moment comes right at the end, just before the last movement. Usually he would have a fast end, but Mozart must have felt that his despair wasn't being heard. He adds an adagio plump with grief, an internal weeping of universal proportions for such small forces. Only after this are we allowed to be happy again, but by now, who could be? The sunshine is gone.

Graham Berkeley was the first violinist. Graham was a superb player for such a young chap. He played sweetly, elegantly and emotionally. All those tragic semitones of Mozart fell under Graham's spell and the rest of us in the quintet just followed along. Graham went on to become a viola player and eventually a software designer in America. He was on the second plane that flew into the twin towers on 11 September 2001. His mum, on hearing of his death, said, 'The sunshine has gone out of our lives.'

By now I'd made it into the youth chamber orchestra in the county. And I was the principal viola player. This meant I had a tiny little team of viola players to look after, making sure we played in the right place and that all our bows were going in the same direction. Harder than it sounds. The summer of my fifteenth year, I went away to music camp. The chamber orchestra had its own rehearsals, but one day the string players were told to go into the big hall and join the symphony orchestra strings. The big kids. This was the musical equivalent of being asked to have tea with God. Suddenly I was sitting among people I had only gawped at from afar; these magnificent creatures impressed not only with their playing, but also with their fashion flair, their intelligence and their beauty. I couldn't believe I was worthy to be close to them, let alone play music with them.

Mr Thirlby was conducting that afternoon and had decided that we should all play J.S. Bach, his Third Brandenburg Concerto in G Major.

I had only played a little bit of Bach in orchestra before, and always school arrangements of his music — *Jesu Joy of Man's Desiring, Air on a G String, Sleepers Wake* etc. School arrangements can be a very convenient way of playing great music in a slightly simpler setting than the original, although the philosophy does have its detractors. Some teachers believe that if you are going to play a piece, you should do it properly, not a pale version of it with only the tune remaining. So when I was presented with the first viola part of the first movement of the Brandenburg, I was petrified. First of all, there were a lot of notes. I mean, really, a lot. Secondly, I knew for an absolute fact that everybody else in the room could play their parts perfectly and I would play at the wrong time and be made to leave the room. Mr Thirlby lifted his baton, with the supposedly inspiring words:

'Just get the beginning and end right, and the middle will look after itself.'

I didn't and it didn't. Few bike crashes have been as hair-raising or out of control, even ones where I broke the frame of my body or my bike. When the weather changes my body aches in memory of those crashes, a shoulder here, an arm there; when I play, indeed even listen to, the third Brandenburg Concerto, there is a slight ache that sits somewhere in my inner viola stomach. An anxiety that the middle will not look after itself.

D major/minor

My first memory of music was its absence. Silence seeped through our low-ceilinged home, most noticeably on Sundays when each of us confined ourselves to our set spaces and tasks. Mum in the kitchen cooking a Sunday roast, the door closed to be alone. Tim drawing in his bedroom. Me playing with toy figures in the garage. Silence seemed obligatory. A bitter divorce takes the music of your happiness away, so why allow music at all?

When we were on school holidays, Mum was at work and Gran'ma had gone home, we discovered the record player. It was a simple pale wooden box, a recluse in the corner, unused since my parents' divorce in 1969 and with records to match. If Miss Havisham had had records and a turntable, this too would have been their story.

Liz, I think, as the oldest, took one of the single records from its slight paper sleeve, turned the dial, took the arm and dropped the needle into the groove. For the first time in my childhood music swung out into the room, swept into my ears and I fell forever in love. Petula Clark singing 'Downtown', singing 'da daa', singing music and rhythm and worry and troubles and forever going downtown. Again and again, Downtown, Downtown, Downtown, joined by Jonathan King going to the moon and Astrud Gilberto smiling. A revelry of LPs and singles that my sisters put on as I sat wondering why this joy didn't happen when Mum was here, when she was alone in the kitchen cooking. Silence seemed wasteful.

Quite a few years later, on one of those Sundays, Mum and I were alone for the morning and I asked if I could put on some music. Instead of a flat and solid no, Mum said yes and I chose Astrud Gilberto, 'The Shadow of Your Smile'. The shadow of a smile when your love is gone. In my defence, I was so attracted to Gilberto's dusky voice singing slightly out of tune that it didn't occur to me how cruel those words were, from an album that Mum had bought during her marriage and kept in her solitude. When I came back into the kitchen my mum was sobbing over the sink, hands in rubber gloves holding a dirty mixing bowl and tears streaming down into the washing-up water. I had never seen anything so sad and I have not since. The memory still makes me cry. It was then that I realised how unfathomably deep music goes.

Many years later I sat in a rehearsal room at the Royal Academy in London with my quartet, playing Mozart to Norbert Brainin.

And he was crying.

Norbert Brainin was the first violinist of one of the world's greatest ever quartets, the Amadeus. For forty years they played together, made hundreds of recordings, toured worldwide and were my heroes. Some teenagers had sweaty, jean-clad heroes, others had sweaty lycra-clad heroes; I had sweaty dinner jacket-clad heroes playing Mozart and Beethoven and Britten. The Amadeus only stopped performing when their viola player, Peter Schidlof, had a heart attack while running. He was the fit-looking one, with a hawk nose and equine face, aristocratic in bearing and a truly elegant musician. Norbert Brainin, in contrast, was small, tubby like Winnie the Pooh, with a sweep of dark hair and a waistline that grew from LP cover to LP cover. Like plump chefs' food, it was comforting to listen to Viennese music played by a man with fat fingers.

So here I was, with a Countess of Munster scholarship to study with the remaining members of the Amadeus at the Academy and we had made one of them cry. We came to the end of the Mozart D Minor Quartet K. 421, looked up at the maestro with his baby-blue tank top stretched tightly over his tummy and he was sobbing, the same sobs my mother had made. You can probably imagine the terror. Were we awful? Did our phrasing upset his perfect Viennese sensibilities? Had his wife died? We all made gestures to balm him, steeled ourselves for the inevitable bad news and he eventually choked out, 'Music is the most important. Never forget, to be a musician is the most important. You nurse people's souls.'

* * *

The middle of things, according to my viola teacher Mr Thirlby, was A-okay if the beginning and end were together. In our family, that didn't really apply. The middle of things in a sibling sense was not A-okay.

Speaking to Mum about Penny in recent years, she has said that things went awry when Penny was three. Penny stole some sweets from a shop, Mum made her say sorry and embarrassed her such that she hoped Penny would never do it again. It didn't work. Penny became a child who stole. A small, ginger-haired, beautiful thief.

Liz was just a year ahead of Penny in school and was consistently ashamed by ginger magpie Penny stealing money and shiny things from the school cloakroom. Nobody hates a thief more than a child does. And if you are the sister of a thief, well, there must be something wrong with you too. Whenever I went into a new class, the teacher would always say: 'Oh, you're *Penny's* sister …', with a worried stress on 'Penny's'. A subtle re-focus.

Mum's eternal worry was that it was her fault that Penny was so naughty; her eternal hope was that Penny would grow out of it. 'It' being a broad, covering word for stealing, not concentrating, staying out too late and generally behaving like a wild cat. To express her unhappiness, Penny stole. Liz had chronic eczema, an unwilling expression of her own. Tim stole too, but he was not in Penny's league. He kept his thefts close to home, nicking money from Mum's purse. And me? I was very, very quiet.

Up to the age of about eleven, I felt that I had worked out a way to be happy. I played my violin and I loved school and my best friend Sophie; I read and read, some dubious things like the Famous Five (I so wanted to be friends with George) and the Secret Seven, but some good things too, like *I Am David*, about a boy who escapes from a prison camp, walks across Europe and finds his mum. I rode my bike most weekends and throughout the summers, down winding roads, dinging my bell at the corners.

Things took a severe turn for the worse when I was in my final year at primary school and Penny was about fourteen. Children devise rituals to try and stop things going wrong in their life; my ritual was that as soon as I got home, I would ask whomever was there where Penny was. One summer afternoon I asked Liz where Penny was; Liz said she didn't know and continued to watch Roy Castle play different instruments on the TV.

Penny didn't come home. Tim did. Penny didn't come home. Mum did. Penny didn't come home.

Penny didn't come home.

Mum called the police. I nearly threw up with anxiety. Liz scratched her eczema-covered hands and Tim didn't appear to care. The police came round. They came to the front door, which nobody did if they knew us. Our house hardly ever had adult men in it, but now it did. Men in sports jackets with thin hair and big bellies. This was to be the first of many visits by these kind, solid policemen. They always tried to have a little chat with me. I was frozen with fear in their presence, but they still smiled at me.

A notice of Penny's disappearance was put in the local paper the next evening, ironically a paper that Penny herself would have delivered. The following day at school, Liz had to suffer the acute humiliation of people having read this.

Our family life went on in some hollow, shattered way for those two nights Penny was missing. Mum was finally told she had run away to London. Gran'ma came round to help look after us and there were a lot of hushed conversations. Liz got her own back on her hideous schoolmates. After one of them had screamed at Liz's eczema-wounded hands and taunted her, Liz cut off her pigtail. Quietly, on the school bus. We were the family that other families talked about over dinner. 'There, but for the grace of God, go we ...'

This was the beginning of nearly three years of absolute hell for my mother, hell for us all. I realise now that Penny must have been going through hell as well. How desperately unhappy must she have been to do these things. Life became all about making sure Penny was not stealing the safety box our pocket money had to be kept in, not stealing our clothes, not stealing our records. These three years were a reign of terror. I was so terrorised and so debilitated during this time that I often thought of killing myself. Hardly a day would go past where I didn't lie on my bed, head under the blankets, hiding from the hideous, often violent rows taking place downstairs. There was no certainty in my world apart from playing the viola and riding my bike. I did both of them on my own because everybody around me let me down, too busy with their own survival. Even my best friend Sophie had left. I was surprised Penny didn't steal my bike or my viola, but the life and the trust from our family was stolen.

Just when things didn't seem like they could get any more desperate, they did.

Mum had noticed that Penny's back wasn't straight. She was taken to the doctor, then the orthopaedist, and diagnosed with scoliosis. This meant that she had to wear something that would probably be construed as child abuse today — a back brace. A big collar around the neck, a metal rod going down to a hefty leather belt. It was intended to straighten Penny, but it only made her more crooked. She refused to wear it. Eventually she agreed to wear it to school, but not if she went out. The most vicious rows were fought over this brace and the state of Penny's back. Penny would hiss and spit, Mum would hit her, I would cower upstairs. To this day I can't listen to anybody shouting without feeling physically sick.

A truce was drawn and we breathed a little more freely for a few weeks. Mum went along to a parent–teacher evening to see how Penny was doing at school. Mum had rarely come back with good news from these evenings, but this time she came back with news that surprised us all.

Penny's classroom teacher said how wonderful it was that Penny's back had got better so quickly, and that she only had to wear her brace on weekends.

A medical miracle, you might think.

Mum confronted Penny. Penny confessed that she had been hiding her brace in a public toilet and then going to school without it on. She would then collect it on her way home.

Mum gave up. Tim also had scoliosis, inherited through Mum from Grandpa. Mum couldn't bear to go through the same violent fights; Tim and Penny have crooked backs.

We had so many visits from gentle policemen over those years, moments of calm when we would be on tiptoe and then it would all start again. One of the more comical moments was when we all were told we had to be at home early that evening, as a child psychologist was coming round to interview us. A man. By this time I associated adult males with trouble. The police. My dad. And now this man. He sat in a chair that he moved from its regular spot (nobody did that), smoked a cigar (nobody did that, at least not at home) and quizzed us about our life (we never spoke about anything emotional). The best bit? Penny never showed up. Not long after that, when Penny was fifteen and I was twelve, Mum gave up for good.

At this point Mum's heart was covered with cracks; those cracks started to break apart with the constant battles and lies, but I think Mum's heart finally broke when she decided that Penny had to go to the children's home.

It had been another anguished time; Penny had run away again. I'd lost count by now. This time she was gone for several days. When she was eventually found, Mum went down to the police station to collect her, but refused to bring her home. She signed her over into state care and our lives improved overnight. Mum made this decision for the good of our family. How could she do this? How could she not? I didn't see Penny for those six months and I didn't want to. Why would I want to see somebody who had been consistently cruel and violent towards me? The only person who visited Penny during that time was Gran'ma. She called the truce between Mum and Penny and cemented her own place in the family as our angel. We all loved Gran'ma deeply for it, despite the fact that Gran'ma had a tough side: she was highly disapproving of Mum having me

(I was a mistake) and, quite a few years later, Gran'ma had her solicitor send a letter to Penny when she failed to repay a debt. There was no fucking around with Tressie. She kept us together, for better or worse.

We all gradually left home. Penny, obviously, first. After she turned sixteen she left the children's home and worked as a nanny in Germany and Greece. I didn't see her for a few years and when I did, I was still scared of her. Penny actually came back to stay with Mum when she was in her twenties, living out those missing years. I was in Hong Kong by then. Liz left to go to college. Tim was asked to leave when he was eighteen and went to live with a gay couple; coincidentally one of the men had been a carer for Penny in the home.

In my penultimate year of school my viola teacher, by now a splendid man called Simon Stace, suggested I go along to the Royal Northern College of Music to take an advice audition. Simon had said he didn't have anything else to teach me, and maybe I should find out if I was good enough to think about music as a career. I hadn't really, until then. I was studying Russian, which I loved, and was thinking about becoming a spy. Or at least studying Russian at university. In fact, I loved Russian so much that when, mid-Cold War, an army sergeant came recruiting at the girls' grammar when we were sixteen, I enquired whether she had been taught to hate the Russians. I was seriously miffed on their behalf. My deputy headmaster was seriously miffed on the army's behalf and gave me detention for cheek. To give myself other options besides becoming a soldier (the uniform *was* pretty stylish) or a double agent (great raincoats), Mum and I travelled up to Manchester by train to go to the college advice audition. Me with my new viola, which Gran'ma had bought me. I was taken up to the warm-up room and Mum was shown around college by Martin, a wide trombonist from Shropshire. Martin was a superb musician who was eventually denied a job with an opera orchestra; he was considered a fire hazard because of his large size and the small size of the orchestral pit.

I went into the warm-up room and got out my viola and my sheet music. I was to be given an accompanist for the audition, so I put the piano music out for him. A sickening feeling shot through me — I had brought all the wrong piano music. For some reason I had only brought the music for the pieces I had been playing the year before, not the current ones. Shit. Shit. Shit. The pianist John came in, I smiled timidly and we went through the music I had both parts for: Vaughan Williams' Suite for Viola and Schumann's Adagio and Allegro. I hadn't played these in over a year, but when we started it felt surprisingly okay. My viola allowed my body to wrap around it, as if it were a newborn baby. It seemed like an almost out-of-body experience. I was concentrating so much, I was completely in the zone.

I walked into the audition room, the room of the head of strings, Eleanor Warren. She had an enormous, alarming reputation. She was small, loud and not entirely welcoming; wrinkled, talcum-powdered and smoking. A little memory of the child psychologist flashed through me; I felt like the hick from the provinces. Eleanor had been a cellist and music producer for the BBC; the story went that she had taught André Navarra, the French cellist, to play the Elgar concerto like an Englishman.

I played. I played, I think, brilliantly. Although I wasn't playing the music I had planned and practised, that almost seemed better. I now knew that I could play the viola well and it didn't really matter what I was playing.

I sat down in front of Eleanor and the viola player Simon Rowland-Jones, a small man, also smoking, his blue eyes massive in his face. He bore a ridiculously strong resemblance to Rowan Atkinson. I felt like I had been playing for *Blackadder*. They asked me what my hopes or intentions were. I said I didn't really know, that that was why I was there. Couldn't they tell me? Eleanor did tell me. She advised me to give up school and come to the college in the next year. They awarded me an A.

Mum was down in the canteen eating with Martin. I ran over to her and told her what they had said. She burst into tears. Happy ones for the first time in my childhood.

My mother, my beautiful, beautiful mother. Without her love, I wouldn't have become a musician, a lover of books, an athlete, an honest person, a moral person or a compassionate one. My mother poured all her life into us four children. She took me to concerts, she came and saw me play at every single concert I ever did as a kid, she encouraged us all in our sport, she taught us all to cook, she taught us to question, she checked our homework, she made us themed birthday cakes, she held us when we cried, she cuddled me in the evening. We sang rounds together and eventually listened to music together. I think of her walking to and from work each day, not taking the bus to save

My mother, Anne. She is about twenty-five here. My partner, Jane, once asked me who I thought was the most beautiful woman in the world. I answered without hesitation, 'My mother.'

money, wearing her old raincoat, her face screwed up against the cold world. I think of her falling asleep in the corner every night, after cooking dinner. Exhausted beyond comprehension. Her ferocious intelligence was under-utilised in a steady job in the civil service, so that she could support us. I think of the times, the years, I didn't understand all that she did for us, and I weep in shame at my own selfishness.

I shook and wobbled my way through the first year of college. I was from a small town, I was a year younger than most people and was suffering a severe lack of self-confidence. Even eating in the canteen, my hands shook. When I had to play for other people, I could hardly bring my bow to the string. For months it was a complete nightmare of anxiety and so far from the joy of playing I had known when I was eight. I began to believe that I had made a terrible mistake, that I should never have been given a place at the college, that I would never be able to play in public again. When I was in what turned out to be the final year of school, I had become so nervous that I had walked off stage in the middle of a performance. The shame of that still has its shadow deep in my viola stomach.

Somehow, it got better. I practised. I practised, I practised four, five, six hours every day. I ate crappy college hall food, snogged yucky trumpeters, lost my virginity and practised. I not only practised the viola, but also the piano for a second instrument. I woke up, practised scales for an hour, had breakfast and went on to practise studies. I played things slowly, I played them a bit faster, I played difficult technical bits until my muscles had learnt the movements automatically, I played just the four open strings of the viola in different parts of the bow loudly, quietly, ferociously. One time I practised my arpeggios (scales with just the main bits left in) so slowly I fell asleep. My life was four walls of a small cell, with just a minuscule window where students would peer in to see who was inside. If you sounded bad they would peer in, if you sounded shit hot they would peer in then bring their friends to peer as well. I practised a phrase until it was exactly how I had shaped it in my head. When I wasn't actually playing the viola, I was playing it mentally. The viola was completely entwined by my body, and I became, ever so slowly, a good viola player.

And so, through work, my confidence stabilised. I took beta-blockers for bigger concerts, gained some confidence and was given more prestigious concerts to play in. The issue of nerves for musicians is something that is rarely discussed and my teacher simply said that I needed to relax. You think? The general feeling about stage fright at that time was that you either got over it or you gave up. If you weren't comfortable on stage, then you didn't deserve to be there. Alexander Technique worked, but nothing helped like popping a beta-blocker. They slow your heart down so that your hands stop sweating and your arms stop shaking. Your brain, also, doesn't go into panic mode. I still get nervous when I play. Put me out in front of ten thousand people to speak and nerves stay in their best form, as excitement. Put a viola into my hand and I will fall over, scared witless. The nerves accelerate from excitement to pure fear. It is a constant stress that has made life as a musician an even greater challenge.

When I was eighteen, in my second year of college, a bald girl with a scarf wrapped around her head asked me if I would like to play in a quartet with her and her friends. Her name was Miranda and she had alopecia, probably because of a birth control pill she was taking. She was part of the dope-smoking set; her boyfriend of the time, Bill, another viola player, used to come stoned to class, with his sheet music stuffed in his inside coat pocket like the form guide for a day at the races. When Miranda invited me to play with her, a judge's daughter called Abigail and a thin, film-star-looking cellist called Catherine, I said I'd think about it. I was playing it cool, but being asked to play in a quartet is really serious, the equivalent to being invited to live with someone, marry them, be their sister and their psychologist all in one go; even if the people who ask you appear marvellous, you still have to be cautious. I thought it over and sent a note via the pigeon holes to Miranda, agreeing to a play-through of a quartet sometime.

We all met at Cath's student house, a mansion filled with well-dressed, rich musicians and foreign university students. Rich in comparison with me. I was one of the few musicians at college whose family circumstances meant I qualified for a full government grant and, true to my bank account, I lived in a mice-riddled terrace at the back of the Manchester City football ground. I ate cabbage and crappy pasta on a daily basis. In Cath's relative luxury, four chairs were gathered, four music stands, four glasses, a bottle of student preservative otherwise known as red wine, and a set of parts for a Mozart quartet.

Playing music with somebody is like taking off your clothes and getting into bed with them. If it is going to work, you have to leave all your inhibitions behind. Leave them in a pile with your clothes and your instrument case.

Thus undressed, we sat down to play.

Mozart is not my favourite composer to listen to (since you're asking, I actually don't really have one … oh okay, Bach), but he is my favourite to play. There is something about his music that seems to reveal your true state as a musician. Not necessarily your technical ability, but your musician heart. If you have tension, hang-ups or sloppiness in your playing, Mozart will exaggerate them, almost as if his spirit hangs still over the music, judging you and teasing you. He will mock you with a line of quavers that need to be played with a perfect curve, but because of a slight indecision or inability on your part, they come out scrambled and ugly. Mozart is BEAUTY. Pure simple beauty. Playing his music can put you in a state of grace. When you are in tune with your playing, and by that I don't mean just in tune intonation-wise, but in tune with your own senses, then Mozart comes out easily, flowing from the sheet music to your fingers. It's almost as if your brain doesn't do any conscious work at all. If there is a conscious process of reading the sheet music, processing it and then it finally coming out of your body, the music will seem gluggy (yes that is a technical term).

The Mozart we played at the beginning was his Prussian Quartet K. 575 in D Major. The quartet was composed only a couple of years before Mozart died and was commissioned by the King of Prussia. The stingy monarch never paid up in full for his music. How galling would that have been! Mozart complained about it to one of his Masonic mates, undoubtedly while they were rolling up their trouser legs. Or not, as they were already above the knee. The quartet and the five others in the six-pack commissioned ended up being called the Prussians anyway. How annoyed would Mozart have been if he had known that? He would have probably drunk several six-packs himself.

The King of Prussia played the cello, so the quartet has a rich, melodic cello part, much more so than earlier Mozart quartets. Not to say that the cello parts are unsatisfactory in other quartets, they just satisfy a different part of the cellist. The good thing for the viola player if the cellist has a lot of the tunes is that the viola gets to play the bass part, while the cello floats away on top. And if you get to play the bass part, you get to steer the phrasing of the music in a much more direct way than playing a middle part. This was an unusual test for a newly born quartet. Would we survive it, or would we go back to our teachers' wombs, waiting for another invitation?

We survived and in this manner we began our life as a quartet. Four young women, each from a very different background. Abigail had lived in London, and was an ex-child TV soap star. She was extroverted and massively insecure. Miranda, whose hair did finally grow back, came from Leeds, with an academic mother and a grandmother to rival mine in beauty. Cath, the cellist, had grown up in Newcastle with her close, supportive family that I envied for many years. We bonded immediately; we became our own family. After a few months even our menstrual cycles were in synch. We spent most of our spare time together practising, falling off our chairs with glee and subconsciously working out our group roles. The viola player in the group often ends up being the diplomat, the one who smooths over small glitches and makes sure the rehearsal does not fall into a heap of vitriol. This was a role I had taken on in my family to some extent, as different members attacked (sometimes physically) each other. The time Liz pushed Tim through a glass door springs to mind for some reason ... so when I played quartets, it was quite natural for me to do this. And usually safer.

If I hadn't agreed to play with these young women when I was nineteen, my life generally and as a musician would have had far fewer delights. These three made me happy, as I had never been before. Of course we had terrible disagreements about how pieces should be played, but the fervour with which we practised and performed and played music and life together transformed my views of it all: how you interpreted a composer's written instructions, the sympathy with which you played with your partners, and the unseeable, un-haveable seriousness of it all. Music was life itself, it travelled and ended within time, was not possible to hold in your hand and therefore was and is endlessly desirable. It all *mattered*, so intensely, and then Miranda would hit my knee with a pestle (why did we have a pestle and mortar at a rehearsal?) and we would laugh until we nearly dropped our instruments. We were enormously fortunate. I think of Doris Lessing in her book *Shikasta*, where she notes the good fortune of artists. Playing quartets is the highest form of music-making for me and there is nothing better than sitting down with your quartet, a bottle of shiraz and playing together for hours. It was, is and always will be my greatest joy (my partner excluded).

The teachers we had at college were gods to us. They preached at the altar of the music stand and we prayed and knelt before them; we meditated on their wisdom; we gave them the offerings of scales, études and concerts. These people from the magical world of music brought tales of other gods, other lands, other times, new ways to think, new words to use in the language of music. Some of them abused that power by seducing their students, but we knew which ones to avoid. We knew that if we did everything our chamber music coach, Dr Chris Rowland, told us to, ours would be the Kingdom of Music.

The strangest, most bewitching teacher was Eli Goren, violinist and chamber music teacher. What sort of man says, 'There are no trees on your fingerboard'? He meant, and I'm sure you have worked this out, that the putting of your fingers on the fingerboard to change the notes was not inhibited by anything; it is indeed a simple motion, finger up, finger down, so just get on with it. How much better, how much more intriguing, though, to say, 'There are no trees on your fingerboard'?

Eli was from Vienna, Jewish, and had managed to move with his brother to Palestine before the Nazis annexed Austria. He eventually came to Britain after the war and spread his spiritual genius as far as he could. He became the concertmaster of the BBC Symphony Orchestra and, as a founding member of the Allegri Quartet, played with William Pleeth, the teacher of Jacqueline du Pré. The dreams of my childhood were slowly coming true; I was getting closer to the world of Jacqueline and free, clear, unimpeded music-making.

I first saw Eli Goren walking down the stairs at college; he had a curious, hyper-loose gait, very rounded shoulders and a baggy face that had shown a lot of emotion in his sixty or so years. His dark eyes came from another world, a world created from sound. Eli Goren taught my quartet about pulse and speed, or tempo.

Composers have loose, beautifully vague ways of indicating the speed at which they would like you to play their music.

Around Mozart's time, Italian terms were used: lento — slow; andante — at a walking pace (mnemonic 'and aunty'. Actually my aunty walked quite quickly, so it didn't work); allegro — quick; vivace — lively; presto — fast, etc. That's all very well, and a guide of sorts, but not exactly precise. In later years composers would use metronome markings, actually writing what speed the beat should happen per minute. Still, there is room for artistic interpretation and that is part of what makes a great or a distinctly average performance of a piece.

We played the Mozart D Major Quartet to Eli one morning. He looked at us, with the northern light of Manchester limping through the window and falling on his ancient face and said, 'The tempo should be your friend.'

If you are fighting against the speed, whether it is too slow or too fast, then the tempo is not your friend. He went on to say that the tempo of a piece is revealed in all its clarity by a particular passage of the music, which you simply cannot play at any other speed. This is another challenge of the musician, to find this passage, which is rarely at the beginning, and identify the speed at which it will work. But speed is not the only thing; there is also the sense of the pulse. Is it an urgent pulse, does it push forward, or is it a pulse which is solid and stalwart, thumping away steadily like a draught horse's heart? Playing something at the same speed, but giving the music a sense of urgency or contemplation, was a matter of where you placed your notes within the framework of the beat. You can push restlessly against the front of the beat, or you can sit back in your favourite armchair and play as if you have your feet up. It's the difference between going at sixty kilometres an hour in fifth gear, or sixty kilometres an hour in second.

In one simple lesson, Eli Goren taught my quartet about speed. So simple. When I have the chance to pass this on and a young face glows with a new awareness, I remember Eli Goren, a face in a cold light, a face from Eastern Europe, who had brought the mystery of Vienna to us young women. And when I cycle up a mountain, I think of Eli as well. Not too fast, not too slow. At just the right tempo, with just the right pedal cadence.

A major/minor

Music needs punctuation. If it didn't have it, it would drone on like, well, like a drone. At school we once had the challenge of adding punctuation to a series of words printed undivided, incessant, wandering in the grammar desert. We guided them to the oasis by adding full stops and commas, bringing sense to the passage. It is the same with music. Composers give you hints, usually clear (Beethoven) or not (Debussy), and then it is up to you, the musician, to add the punctuation. Those hints are called cadences.

Cadences are waypoints in the music, places where you can take a breather, readjust your instrument and hurtle on to the next bit of the adventure. The most definite of them is the perfect cadence. Think of the end of a Beethoven symphony. A perfect cadence has the biggest tension between the two chords.

In comparison, a plagal cadence sounds almost apologetic. Think of a hymn (it's also known as the 'Amen' cadence). There is an imperfect cadence, when the composer is just hanging around on the street corner, but not stopping for a chat, and then there's the surprise one, the interrupted cadence, where you are heading down a very clear and obvious path and suddenly, whoosh, you have done a ninety-degree turn and you have no idea what is going to happen next or where you will go. This is my favourite.

So, what does happen when you get on a pushbike in England and point it towards Hong Kong? When you make an interrupted cadence?

I had stayed with my mum in Shrewsbury in the weeks leading up to my departure, using the time to finish my preparations. I had gone down to London with Liz to buy camping things and a Canadian sun hat. (Do brown bears get sunburnt?) And I had had my bike upgraded with new gears and brakes by Mr Jones, the man Dad had bought my racer from all those years ago. The new gears were, importantly, not too light, not too fancy. Mr Jones chose well because they are still on my bike tens of thousands of kilometres later. Gone was the old art of finding the gears, though. No more silence of the sliding cable, now it was all index-linked. Click, click, click with my thumbs. I had gone from playing a fretless instrument to playing a fretted one. After two weeks of gear-changing my thumbs were overworked and I couldn't play the violin for a while.

I set off on a Friday. The night before, Penny had made a delicious farewell dinner of my favourite English food, finishing with jelly and chocolate blancmange. After I had got ready and put on a T-shirt that said 'Journey to the East' in Chinese, I stood and looked at myself in the mirror for a long time. It was a summoning and joining of forces gathered through the thirty-two years of my life.

I wanted to not be rank and file any more.

It was the end of September, the beech hedges I had driven past with Gran'ma were at the beginning of their autumn showing-off and the fields outside Shrewsbury were being put to their winter bed. I nearly got run over and killed twice on the first day. As I left Mum's house, with she and Liz and Liz's son Lawrence waving me off, a couple walked past us. As I struggled up my first hill, they asked where I was going.

I had the most enormous pleasure in saying, 'To China.'

Our lives are full of interrupted cadences, full of moments when the direction is changed. Sometimes it is subtle, sometimes it is horrendous, sometimes it takes hindsight to see these moments for what they are. Sometimes one tiny change, seen from a big distance, makes a huge difference. Point that bicycle not quite at Hong Kong and you won't get there.

And sometimes an interrupted cadence can be a joy.

When I was sixteen I went down to Bristol with Mum and my mate Julia to audition for the National Youth Orchestra of Great Britain. I had heard the orchestra on the radio, at the Proms, and a few of the players in Shropshire had been members. This was elite stuff and I played my little heart out. I got in. Julia didn't.

I was sent a pile of music and a list of do's and don'ts, which included the depth of black in your trouser pockets. We played an entire Richard Strauss program with Norman Del Mar, wondering all the time which of his trembling movements was actually the downbeat and then, in the summer, the orchestra met up again to play Mahler and Debussy with Simon Rattle at the Proms.

I was sixteen, I'd had one kiss and during these three weeks my musical life had an interrupted cadence — Simon Rattle made the connection between music and sex. Actually, music and sensuality. We were rehearsing Debussy's *Jeux* and he couldn't get the sound he wanted in a particularly delicate bit. He was dressed in olive green and his hair only had a very few of those glorious white hairs. He looked at us (it felt like he was looking directly at me) and told us to imagine stroking the thigh of someone we fancied.

A hall full of hormone-drenched teenagers, and Simon Rattle has just given us permission to make love to each other. I wish I could show here the sound we made at that moment. Nothing could have captured it; it was so strong, you could smell it. Definitely an interrupted cadence. Music has never been the same for me since.

As well as the *Games* with Debussy, we played Mahler's Symphony No. 6 in A Minor, 'The Tragic'.

It's a work that seems to sprawl over centuries and continents. The symphony opens with the low strings stamping a military march through the ages, with shrill cries from trumpets and heckles from oboes. It is a hideous call from hell. The last movement alone is as long as Brahms' Fourth Symphony. Although the work is for full symphony orchestra, much of it is scored for little, sad, wistful ensembles, a flute and a violin here, a horn and timpani there. There are cowbells and twisted, crippled dances from Mahler's dreams and, in the final movement, a curse that awaits the optimistic conductor.

Mahler had put three blows of fate in the score. These are stunning musical and dramatic moments, but you need to do two different things for the music and the drama. For the musical effect, a plank of wood is allowed to slam down onto the floor, creating a slap that brings death and utter vacuity in its wake. There is no hope after you hear this sound. However, for the dramatic effect, the audience needs something to see, something which will match this desolation, so often the lucky percussionist gets to use an almost joke-sized hammer and slams it down onto a wooden box. Tom and Jerry meets Gustav Mahler.

Poor hapless, miserable Gustav, who forever linked the misery of his parents arguing to the sound of a hurdy-gurdy playing on the street. Mahler eventually felt that the three blows of fate were one too many. He had many misfortunes in his life; having to leave the Vienna State Opera due to anti-Semitism, the death of his oldest daughter, and the heart condition which would eventually kill him. So to tempt fate by playing all three hammer blows … well, he chose not to. When we played the finale with Rattle, he chose to go along with Mahler's eventual wishes and left out the final hammer blow. What is left is even more gut wrenching: unresolved tension. Leonard Bernstein described this symphony as 'the catastrophe of *Homo sapiens* itself'. You find yourself, as a listener and as a player, wandering through the mountains, among the cowbells and twisted, broken children, desperate to believe that hope is still there, even though everything in the world tells you it is not. These alpine meadows are strewn with major chords that turn, even without pausing, into minor ones. From flowers to skulls. In some corners of the meadows there is a distant nostalgia that provides a moment of calm, but then the horror returns. That major chord always turns into a minor one. Always.

When I decided to cycle to Hong Kong, I think I wanted to take control of things. Minor chords seemed to dominate in my life. When I told my parents what I was going to do, my dad, John Ernest George, told me to get enough sleep and to not be afraid to give up. My mum said that I was selfish and burst into tears.

The first few days were pretty horrible physically. My little violin case rubbed a sore into my spine, and I had to shove a sock behind my bra strap to stop it. My arse killed and so did my wrists. I was twenty kilos or so overweight and hills in Shropshire and the Cotswolds and in Kent are sharp little buggers. I couldn't wait to get down to the bottom of England, to be away from my homeland, to be 'somewhere else'. A teenage boy laughed shrilly as I climbed a hill into a town one afternoon and the sky remained low, heavy and hopeless. I fell headfirst into a ford in the back lanes of Oxfordshire, just as I was thinking, 'Must make sure I don't fall headfirst into that ford …' Finally, after a miserable week where I watched a friend watch his girlfriend slip towards her death from bowel cancer, I caught the ferry in

Folkestone and watched the White Cliffs from the back of the boat. I was born on those cliffs and, as the ferry entered the waters of the English Channel, I was re-born.

You know you've arrived 'somewhere else' when men smoke at petrol stations. And when policemen shout 'Courage!' at you as you cycle the route of the Monaco Grand Prix. And when you get stuck on an elevated motorway in Genoa and you don't get arrested, the police merely shrug and suggest you shouldn't be there.

One of the down and up sides of long-distance cycling is getting a little lost. Actually, I am reasonably proud to say I only got really lost once, in Iran. There were other times in towns, trying to find the right road to leave on, but only once did I get really and truly lost. The kind of lost when you start to sweat a little, and your stomach begins to clench and you begin to think panicked, 'I've watched too much scary TV' thoughts.

I was trying to get from Astara, right on the Azerbaijan–Iran border, to Rasht, along the Caspian Sea. Everything had been going so easily those last few days and I had even had a brief diversion, a fling with a beautiful young Norwegian man. The day after, I had gone to the swimming pool and swum naked with other women, feeling the warm water between my legs and thinking quite practically about the complete lack of desire I had for men. On the bicycle again and bang, one little lack of concentration and I was on the wrong road, going south instead of east. It's easy to navigate on a journey if you're always going in the same direction (which was basically east) and so I had become complacent. After an hour or so, about twenty-five kilometres, I realised that the sun was in the wrong place. I checked the map, my compass, and thought the map must be wrong. Maybe the Iranians didn't want foreigners cycling round their country, so they sold them dodgy maps in the hope they would give up. This was the stupid panicked thinking starting. It was getting late. The sun, now firmly to the right of me, was going down. I had maybe two hours left of twilight and then I would be a lonely, solitary, did I say lonely, woman on a bike in the middle of a very scary desert. I turned round.

The feeling that night, when I got into Rasht, was one of total triumph. I had put my head down and cycled at a cadence and tempo that I felt I could just about put up with for forty kilometres. I shoved dates into my mouth, hitched up my ridiculously long coat that I was obliged to wear (no lycra for ladies in Iran) and willed myself to Rasht. When I arrived the city lights were on, made even more twinkly by the dark of the Caspian Sea in the distance and the looming of mountains to the south. Assassins had their castles there once. I celebrated with ice-cream. In hindsight, I realised that being lost was quite invigorating, in a life-threatening kind of way.

The first time I got lost in a piece of music was playing Shostakovich's Festive Overture. I was about thirteen and had been dragged into the big students' orchestra in music camp. I sat down next to an eighteen-year-old called Ruth who was a beautiful viola player and studied Russian with the same teacher as me at school. She was dark and clever and kind, and I really wanted to *be* her. Mr White, our conductor, dressed in his regular safari suit (who needs a jungle when you have classical music?), brought in the trumpets with their fanfare. The viola part moved off at a steady pace and I managed to hold on for a few bars, but soon the orchestra began to move away from me and panic set in. This only got worse as the piece moved from the relative calm of the opening to a brisk, new gear. The clarinets flew by, the notes on the page flew by even quicker and I got horribly, hopelessly lost. The sickening feeling of being lost in the Iranian desert was nowhere near as bad as getting lost in Shostakovich's crotchets and minims. Ruth was very kind and occasionally pointed her bow quickly at where we were in the piece. I think I caught the last few bars and just about managed to stop playing at the right time. It took me many years to realise that being lost is all right. And the most difficult thing is accepting you *are* lost. It's a bit like cycling in the rain: once you accept you are going to get wet, it's one of the most beautiful things in the world. And after all, if you're lost you are just somewhere you didn't plan to be and that means an adventure is in store. Or at least a good story.

It's easy to feel a little lost in life when there is nothing to look forward to, nowhere special to point your compass towards. I love my job, don't get me wrong, but after doing breakfast radio for a few years I thought there was something more I could be doing, something more I could be contributing. Sitting in a studio *talking* about classical music sometimes seems too hemmed in. I wanted to make music, teach music.

So I went looking for an adventure. Subconsciously at first, then consciously as I looked at people I admired and saw how they travelled in the world and seemed to have no limits. This adventurous line of thought resurfaced on Anzac Day, as I was looking for music stories from places around the world where Australian forces are currently serving. I just put 'music' and 'Kabul' into the search engine and my computer seemed to play a fanfare, a festive overture of stories about the Afghanistan National Institute of Music in Kabul. There were many stories on newspaper sites around the world about a remarkable man, Dr Ahmad Sarmast, and his quest to re-establish music in his country after the years of silence under the Taliban.

When the Taliban entered Kabul in September 1996, apparently the first place they went to was the musicians' part of town. The Mujahideen before them had done a pretty thorough job of destroying the quarter, but the Taliban went even further and killed and imprisoned the musicians they found practising. They smashed instruments. By the time the Taliban were overthrown, only three traditional instruments belonging to Radio Kabul remained, and only due to them being buried. The thought of an instrument, any instrument, being destroyed, is horrifying to most people. It is like tearing humanity's heart out, a war on music. Is that what Jimi Hendrix, Pete Townshend, Keith Moon and others were intending? Did they think of the kids who didn't have a guitar, or a drum kit, when they so egotistically smashed theirs on stage? Is there not a guitar god who gives you only a limited number of guitars in your lifetime? It brings to mind the Cultural Revolution in China and the treatment of musicians then. The only so-called music that was allowed to be performed in those times was opera by Madame Mao, among others. When I was playing in the orchestra in Hong Kong I had commented to a fellow viola payer, Mr Yu, about how many times we had played a certain Beethoven symphony that season. Mr Yu gave me a sympathetic and at the same time withering look. He had played in the opera company in Shanghai during the Cultural Revolution and had had to play Madame Mao's opera for more than ten years. Eight times a week. There was one passage he never played correctly. That was his protest.

I wrote to Dr Sarmast. I stated my viola and radio credentials and asked if I could come and do a little teaching and some interviews. He welcomed me and so I ended up travelling to Kabul in January 2013. A diplomat who officially advised me against going also said unofficially, 'Go now. In ten years' time people will be amazed that there was ever a music school in Kabul.'

The courage of the students at the music school moved me more than anything ever has. Their simple desire to make music counted for more than anything. As one Afghan musician said, the only thing they feared was God.

Playing music requires you to be fearless. This was dripped, shaken, pressed and sometimes violently shoved into me by Christopher Rowland at the Royal Northern College. Chris died a few years ago, after battling cancer for a cruelly long time. He had played in the Fitzwilliam Quartet as first violinist and had premiered many of Shostakovich's quartets in the West. Chris was a teacher of huge importance, because he taught us young musicians to feel and to make others feel. He coaxed and heckled and whispered our deepest emotions from us. One time he told us that we had to sound as happy as I looked when I was cycling. One of Chris' great legacies, beyond quartets he brought together like the Elias and the Navarra, is the recording of Beethoven's Quartet in A Minor Op. 132.

Beethoven had been severely ill just before he composed this; the music was his way of saying thanks to his God for his recovery. Ludwig was ill many times in his life, mostly a terribly painful stomach affliction that began in his twenties.

Two of the students at the Afghanistan National Institute of Music and two of the bravest young women I have ever met. Fearless, strong, best of friends.

People still don't really know what killed Beethoven in the end. Was it lead from the wine he drank? Was it hepatitis? Was it the composers' disease, syphilis? Whatever it was, the disease was long, yet gave moments of reprieve. And those moments we can be thankful for, along with Beethoven, because they gave us this quartet.

The piece includes a slow movement headed 'A Convalescent's Holy Song of Thanksgiving to the Divinity'. The movement is marked molto adagio, or at a speed that is extremely comfortable. There is no haste in it and a performance of this part alone takes about twenty minutes. The movement starts with the first violin playing two notes rising a major sixth, then dropping a tone. Just as they do, the second violin, then the viola, then the cello do the same thing. It gives a cumulative effect of gratitude. Gratitude for life, gratitude for this short reprieve, gratitude for humanity and gratitude above all for music. All this comes from these few notes. The piece sums up music for me. And those musicians in Afghanistan were the equivalent in human terms. Their bravery and gratitude gave me a new lease on life and I realise now that meeting them was an interrupted cadence.

E major/minor

E major is the sunshine key. When you hear those four sharps on a string instrument and feel the tautness of the vibrations, your spirits immediately get a little shot of happiness.

Things were coming along nicely on my trip. My thumbs were recovering from my bike gears and I had made it all the way to Paris. This was the mythical beginning of my trip from all those months ago, when I had talked to my American friend Chris about doing it in the first place, so being in Paris seemed extra special. I met up with Cath, from my student quartet, who was now a bigwig cellist with John Eliot Gardiner's band. She was playing in an opera with him at the Comedy Theatre (although the opera was a tragedy) and we hung out for a few days. Cath is sartorially splendid and my fleece and cycling trousers didn't pass muster, especially in Paris; with scorn and pity for the travelling cyclist she lent me some of her clothes and took me out to the suburbs to listen to her, Steven Isserlis' sister Annette and somebody else play quartets with Ivry Gitlis.

A critic once gave Ivry Gitlis the greatest accolade: he or she said, after hearing him play Franck's Violin Sonata, that they couldn't decide whether it was the best or the worst interpretation they had ever heard. Ivry lived in a farmhouse just outside Paris, so we took the train and were picked up at the station by Michael Stern, Isaac Stern's son.

The four went inside to play Mozart and I was left to play with Michael's daughter in the orchard. It was autumn and the apples were ripening and dropping off the trees. The six-year-old, whose name now escapes me, asked me if she could pick an apple. So I lifted her up, higher and higher, until her fingers wiggled their way onto one of the fruit. The sun glinted over the barn and I made a silent promise to Isaac that I wouldn't drop his granddaughter. She leapt down, took a bite of the apple and threw it to the ground. Mozart was calling from the music room.

As I rode down through France, I was quite enjoying the relative easiness of playing the violin, especially a three-quarter size one, after the viola. A viola's body is about sixteen and a half inches long, but my little violin was only twelve. It's right over there now, in the corner by the music cabinet. I don't play it much any more as I went back to the viola and on to the cello, but sometimes I get her out, tune her up and play a bit of Bach. Mr and Mrs Skylark's posher cousins made her and she has a chestnut varnish and really sounds quite good for $200. Each night I would arrive at a little hotel, tuck my bike into bed, go out and buy some cheese (Époisses is my favourite), come back and do some practice. Well, perhaps practice isn't quite the right word. Practice is playing with enormous detail and consistently analysing your progress. I had done that for years and now I just wanted to enjoy playing through stuff. I wanted to do what it had taken me years to learn *not* to do. So that's what I did. I opened up my little miniature copy of the Bach Sonatas and Partitas and worked my way through them, from the high drama of the beginning G Minor Sonata to the utter delight of the E Major Partita. I would stop on the way and attempt the 'Chaconne', but frankly there were always the most complaints from other hotel guests whenever I tried that. If I wanted to feel calm and secure, I played the slow movement from the C Major Sonata, but if I needed a fizz of delight, I turned to the back and the E Major Partita Prelude.

The prelude starts with a cheeky little moment's silence; the first note comes on the offbeat and hurtles down a baroque staircase to the middle of the violin, where the notes are thrown around in a tumble dryer. Then they all leap up an octave, as if this time they are poking their tongue out at the wimps down below. It always makes me think of little kids romping in the playground, endlessly moving and taunting and jousting and laughing. Then they all join hands and spin and spin and spin until they get so dizzy they fall apart, and start the whole thing again. It's a fun ride like no other and riding the hills and valleys of this music brought me slowly back to loving playing again.

The tempo of the prelude made a big difference to whether I played it well or really quite badly. If I headed off with too much enthusiasm and not enough circumspection, the notes quickly gobbled up little Aurelia and me, and we had to stop. I was learning the same thing with cycling. Climbing over the Apennines in Italy had been my first really big challenge. I managed to cross them just before the first snow of the year came, but if I set off too quickly after each coffee stop the physical action very soon became arduous and unenjoyable. I know it might seem strange that climbing a bloody great big mountain could ever be enjoyable, but if you have the right gear and the right pedal cadence, you are at the top before you know it. Well, before you want to give up, at least. My cycling became smoother and my pedal stroke lighter and quicker. As my prelude improved, so did my travel.

I had arranged with my sister Penny to send my passport back to England when I arrived in Greece, so that she could send it on to the Iranian, Pakistani, Indian and Chinese embassies to get the visas. The only problem with cycling is the issue of when to apply for your visa, and whether it will still be valid by the time you arrive at the country. It had taken me a while to work out that I would need to be without my passport for a time, in order to get the visas at the right time. So I had filled in all the necessary forms before I left and put them in an envelope for Penny to send off to various agents.

Visas were a constant worry for me. Europe was all easy, as I was British back then, but before I started my trip I travelled down to London to visit various embassies and check the viability of being allowed into their countries. The Pakistanis gave me no reason for hope. I walked into their High Commission and sat down to wait for my turn. The room was dark and brown and seemed to have been lifted directly from Pakistan, air and smell (spicy) included. I was eventually called up to a counter and spoke to a middle-aged, bored-looking man who asked me when I was travelling, where I was travelling and how I was travelling. When wasn't a problem, but where and how; well, then the difficulties began. I stated that I would be arriving at the border with Iran, then leaving the country at the top of the Karakoram Highway, at the border with China.

'And how will you be travelling?' the clerk asked. His eyes were beginning to pop a little, as I had also had to admit I would be travelling alone.

Sisters in Greece, at their small hotel. They looked after me like a daughter and were quite disapproving of me cycling on my own. Just like my ol' ma.

'By bicycle.'

The clerk shouted out across the whole office, 'This lady is going to travel the *whole* of Pakistan … by bicycle!'

The place erupted with laughter. This was the first, but I hope not the last, time I have been laughed out of an embassy. I decided to go through an agent. On my Iranian and my Pakistani forms I simply forgot to say that I was travelling by bicycle. Woops.

So I was in Rhodes, waiting for my passport to come back, kind of killing time a little. I ended up being there for a week or so, cycling round the island, looking at the way life was governed by things you caught in nets (fish and olives), going to see films, sort of living there, in a brief way. One evening I was walking back from a movie and I glanced into a shop where the light was on right at the back. It was a very long watchmaker's shop and I could just about see a man at the back sitting on his own, playing the violin. By now I had learnt that the best way to have an adventure, however small, is to talk to people, so I knocked on the door. The man looked up from his music, I waved, and he walked to the door and opened it.

'I'm sorry to bother you, but I also play the violin. May I listen?'

Which is a kind of odd thing to say, in a way, isn't it? I mean, lots of people play the violin. I live in Sydney and if I saw somebody here play the violin I wouldn't necessarily go and talk to him or her. Maybe I should. Maybe we should live our lives as if we are away from home. Anyway, thanks to George and his good humour, he invited me in to his shop. His name was George Trikilis and he spoke beautiful Australian. He took me down to the violin-playing end of the watch shop and told me his story.

George had been a violinist for a long time. He was from a very poor family, a peasant family, but he used to play in a band to help out. He got fed up with people paying him by licking money and sticking it on his head and decided to move to Australia instead. He was given an immigration visa in the seventies and used his last drachmas to buy some trousers for the very long, very hot plane trip. The trousers he had bought were cheap and blue. The air-conditioning on the plane was broken and George was frightened of flying, so he didn't get up to walk around for all those hours. When he finally arrived in Brisbane, the seat of his trousers was white, and the white of the seat was blue. He had to wear these trousers for the next few months until he could afford some new ones. People told him he looked like a white-bottomed human baboon.

George was a delightful host. He gave me wine and olives and we talked for a long time about the violin and Australia. He had decided to leave in the end; he couldn't stand the racism he experienced. So he had come back to Rhodes and seemed happily unhappy. George had a big birthmark over his face, which must have been a difficult thing to grow up with. His character was defiant and he played the violin like that. Relentless and stubborn. I went back the next night and we greeted each other like old friends, drank more wine and played duets into the small hours. The next day my passport arrived with all the visas in it, so I caught the boat to Turkey. George has been such a happy presence in my mind now for all these years. I wish he had come back to Australia.

George was the beginning of a long hospitable line, stretching all the way across Turkey, Iran, Pakistan and China; a line of kind people. In Muslim countries in particular, I was welcomed in every town, invited into homes, and paid for, fed and even pyjama-ed. I gave whatever I could to them, even if it was only an English lesson.

In Tabriz, Iran, I was stopped in the street and asked by a young woman if I was a foreigner. It must have been the shoes that gave me away, but I ended up being invited into Rahime's home. She was an English teacher and, while her mother cooked a perfect lamb stew called abgusht, Rahime quizzed me about certain English phrases. Many Iranians have illegal

The marvellous George Trikilis. Whenever I pass shops in the evening now I always look in, hoping to find a violinist at the back, practising.

satellite dishes to watch foreign TV and Rahime had obviously become quite attached to the cops and robbers channel.

'What is the meaning of "the coast is clear"? And how about "the game is up"?'

Then, in a different genre completely, 'What is the meaning of "an Englishman's home is his castle"?'

What, indeed. After abgusht, we played cards with her mother and brother. They thrashed me in a game that they didn't teach me the rules for, which I thought was a bit rough, then they asked me to teach them a game back. I said there was one game, but it would take about a lifetime to learn (Bridge), so I compromised and we played Snap. They loved it.

This hospitality continued throughout Iran. The roads were really excellent, good surface and gradient, and each day I was able to cycle about one hundred and fifty kilometres quite easily. This did mean that I needed to eat a lot, though. The regular, roadside café fare was a simple chicken kebab with tomatoes and onion, yoghurt, rice and a slice of orange. It was beautiful food, always so clean and well cooked, but it simply wasn't enough. So after one long morning I pulled into a restaurant, which was being repainted on the outside, went in and ordered my regular kebab. It was brought very promptly to me, I scoffed it down and I was still so hungry I immediately ordered another, exactly the same. The man laughed at me, then, when I went to pay, he refused to take my money.

'No, you are our guest.'

His name was Hovasan. He invited me to stay with him and his family, but I still wasn't quite used to accepting such warmth, so I declined. I had to laugh when I went outside to collect my bike; the two very burly restaurant painters were riding around the courtyard on her. Vita still has a smear of blue paint on the handlebars.

In Kashan, Iran, there is a magical, traditional house, called the Abbasian House, preserved now as a museum. I visited there one morning and a man who I didn't know, who expected nothing from me, paid my very expensive foreigner's entry fee for me. He then showed me into the house and quietly disappeared. The house was built in the late 1700s, with 1700s air-conditioning. Although this was March and only about twenty degrees in the daytime, you could still tell that the air-conditioning was brilliantly effective. The air was collected from openings in the

How do you like my headscarf? In Iran, with the generous restaurant owner who wouldn't let me pay for two meals I'd just scoffed. One of the restaurant painters took this photo.

roof and funnelled down through cooling adobe into the main rooms (for readers younger than thirty who only know adobe as a software company, it's a traditional building material). There were rooms that were cooler than others, light, airy rooms, balconies, a theological courtyard and then, the most beautiful room I have ever seen — a room of stars. This open chamber had a fireplace, and the curved walls and ceiling were covered with tiny mirrors in the shape of stars and the moon. The effect at night, when the mirrors reflected the fire, must have been staggering.

I wandered out into the garden, drugged by the beauty I had just seen. I sat down on a low wall and looked around at the perfect balance of greenery, water channels and shade. Even the garden's sound was cooling. A gaggle of schoolgirls, all keen to practise their English, sidled over to me.

'What is your name?' asked one girl, pointing at me.

'What is your name?' she said again, pointing at herself, then answering 'Azeen!'

One man's gesture of lending me his pyjamas sums up the hospitality on this journey. I had arrived at a tiny little town called Anar, about one hundred and twenty kilometres from Yazd. It was the Iranian New Year, Nowruz, and I was anxious about the only hotel being closed for the holiday. The hotel man in Yazd had assured me it would be open, but I suspected he was just telling me the thing I wanted to hear. I arrived in Anar, found the hotel, the one hotel, and it was closed. A crowd gathered as I stood there in my baby blue headscarf and long shirt, dusty and sweaty from the ride. What should I do? There was no way

Schoolgirls in Iran. I was there in March and it was already hotting up. I can't imagine wearing these black, heavy chadors and shoes in their summer ...

I could return to Yazd. Maybe I should find a mosque, or go to the police? I faltered and tried to look nonchalant. A man with greying hair, holding the hand of a very small, wild-eyed boy, came up to me and told me the hotel was closed for the holiday. He must have noticed the flicker of panic cross my face as he very quickly, in simple English, said I could come home with him and stay the night with his family.

It really is impossible to say how we make decisions in times like these. Often people have been trusting and have been fooled. The only thing I remember about this instantaneous choice was that he had kind eyes, and he had a child. Not exactly concrete evidence. I know that there are terrible stories of kidnap and murder, but the fact is, moments of kindness are SO much more common, yet they don't stick in our minds. I chose to believe in kindness and I still do. This whole trip proved to me that we are simply, overwhelmingly kind.

I followed Ahmad home, cycling behind him in his Hillman Hunter. His wife was naturally rather surprised to have an English cyclist to cater for that night, but she took it in her stride and also took the opportunity to invite all her cousins round to meet me. After more abgusht we went for a drive around the town and Ahmad's wife lent me her spare chador. And when it was time to go to bed, Ahmad insisted I sleep in their bed and he lent me his blue pyjamas.

E major may be the key of bright sunshine, but E minor is an introspective key, an autumnal key, melancholic, quiet and subtly lit. You need to go to it, rather than have it come to you. It is the key Elgar chose for his cello concerto, written in 1919. This was one of the pieces I had heard Jacqueline du Pré play when I was eight; it had left a huge impression on me. Even without seeing the intensity with which she played, just from listening to the record, I was struck by an immense desire to play this music, so when my mum put me down for the violin a little proto-cellist in me died. There is a viola version of the cello concerto, transcribed by the great viola player Lionel Tertis, but to be frank it's just not as good on the viola. My mum bought me the sheet music for it when I was about sixteen. I was excited to play the opening chords, the low E on the C string bolstering the higher notes of the minor chord. The angst of the music was there, but as hard as I tried, I just couldn't get it to sound how I heard it in my head. I think Mum was a bit disappointed. I think maybe she wanted me to sound more like a cellist. Maybe she felt guilty for not following my wishes all those years ago.

Listening to du Pré play it again now and watching her on YouTube, I am still stunned by the complete immersion she had in that piece. Her timing and urgency in the opening chords, her gracious passion in the slide down to the bottom E and her sense of nobility in the melody have never, to my mind, been equalled. My student quartet was lucky enough to have some lessons with William Pleeth, her teacher for so many years, and he talked to us a little about Jacqueline. He said that everybody thought that she did everything naturally, that she never had to work at anything. Actually there were some things she did find hard, particularly fast string-crossing. Mr Pleeth then said how easy it is, you simply wave goodbye with your bow hand. After that tiny window into the world I had dreamed and thought so much about, he brought us back to reality. Standing there, in his crisp shirt and cravat, he waved an arthritic finger at Miranda the second violinist and me and said, 'Now, you two, play louder. I like my quartets to come from the middle.'

The lure of the cello stayed with me over decades. I would ask friends if I could play on their cellos, I would more eagerly go to cello concerts than viola ones, my ear would be endlessly drawn to the cello line in quartets. When I stopped playing viola professionally I began to think about whether I should try to officially learn the cello. It would be such a lot to give up, though. I would have to stop playing the viola to give my brain and hands a chance to reshape themselves and really, at thirty-two, what chance did I have of becoming any kind of a cellist? How much did I simply love playing music and how much did I want to be accomplished at an instrument? If I did begin the cello, maybe I would end up being stuck in a purgatory of neither being a cellist nor a viola player. I wasn't prepared to cross over. Not yet.

B major/minor/
C flat major/minor

To travel from E major to B major, you need only the addition of an A sharp. It is one small step for musicians, but one giant leap for music because we have now arrived in a strange, new world. This is the world of enharmonic keys. Before you begin to skip this bit because of the use of the word 'enharmonic', I'll try to explain.

Accepting that there are twelve semitones in an octave, notes can be called different names depending on which key you are in. For instance, B can also be called C flat. B and C are a semitone apart. F sharp can be called G flat. A flat can be called G sharp. These are called enharmonic notes. In the same way, you can have enharmonic keys.

When you look at a piano keyboard, you see black notes between the white ones. If the keyboard were to be truly in tune, a mere single black note would not be enough. You would need several, subtly different pitches, depending on the key you are in.

Back in the old days, pre-J.S. Bach, the keyboard had to be tuned to fit a particular key and its nearest relations. If you were starting off in C major, the keyboard would be pretty well in tune for G and D major, but go any further and it would start to sound pretty sour and out of tune. The reason for this is a practical joke that I blame on God. The universe has played a special trick on musicians; you see, if every note is precisely in tune with all the other ones, and the other ones are all in tune with each other, then they don't all fit into an octave. It's the musical version of sardines and there is always about a quarter of a tone that gets squeezed out. Around Bach's time and even as far back as the 1500s and Galileo's dad Vincenzo, musicians and theorists were trying to work out how they could have acceptable intonation and not have to retune their lute and keyboard every time they changed keys. There are lots of different ways of doing this now, shave a little off a note here, a little there, and the result is what you hear these days on a piano. Nothing is truly in tune, but for most people it is enough in tune.

Intonation itself can be subjective. If I find myself in a slightly bad mood, it takes me much longer to tune my viola. And where you place notes in a scale might seem simple, but it is the work of a lifetime for some — every morning Pablo Casals, the great cellist, sat down with his cello and played open C, first finger D then third finger E. It was the E he said he never really knew where to put, that problematic major third.

So on keyboards, and on fixed-pitch instruments such as percussion, we have ended up with tempered pitch; it means that when you play in B major on the piano, it sounds exactly the same as if the composer had written in C flat major. On the piano then, it makes no difference to the sound, but if you were playing these keys in a string or wind ensemble, the two would sound quite different. These instruments have the ability to make a B major world sound different from a C flat major world.

It's important to remember that this enharmonic key business only applies to Western music. The Indian raga system and the Middle Eastern maqam system don't have the same problem with this physical conundrum because they are melodic forms of music, rather than harmonic, and there is a movable tonic, or home note. Western classical music is built on chords, a constant vertical relationship, but go further east and the music becomes more horizontal.

In the 1800s the two systems met with the introduction of the harmonium into India by French missionaries. Many Indians thought this new instrument was marvellous: easy to play, nice and loud so you could accompany yourself singing, and fairly light (have you ever tried carrying a sitar in its case?). And you could also teach yourself and not have to enter the exclusive teacher/student world of music family dynasties. For purist Indian musicians, though, the harmonium was a disaster. Indian music, instead of twelve semitones in an octave, has twenty-two shrutis, much smaller intervals, and because the harmonium's twelve notes in an octave were a fixed pitch, it meant you could not do the slides and tiny pitch changes that were necessary in Indian music according to which raga you were playing. The purists hated the harmonium so much that as soon as possible they had it prohibited. All-India Radio banned the harmonium from broadcast in 1940 until 1971.

It's a penumbral place we are now in, among the enharmonic keys. There are six of them, including the minors. What I love about these keys is that it is all about perspective. Sometimes, even if a piece is written in a certain key, it can be easier to occasionally flip your mind to think in the enharmonic key for a moment.

Border towns seem penumbral to me in the same way. Neither quite still the country you are leaving, nor yet the country you are going to. They are places that seem to float in the world, belonging to their own state of crossing.

I was worried about my journey to Dogubeyazit, the eastern border town leading from Turkey to Iran. Snow had come with a vengeance to the Anatolian plateau. In my planning I had completely underestimated how severe the weather could be, so instead of freezing to death on the road I decided to take an overnight bus from the middle of Turkey to the border. My bike was carefully stowed underneath and I got into the bus, modern and plush, with a young man sitting next to me. He was silent and respectful and when we stopped for food, he gave me half his doner kebab. I knew we were starting to arrive in the Kurdish area in the morning as the police stopped the bus a number of times, checked people's IDs and were extremely rude to the young men, including my lovely doner donor.

We finally arrived in Dogubeyazit. I pulled Vita and my entire luggage from the underneath of the bus, waved goodbye to my Kurd in shining armour and marvelled at this new landscape. Where I had been the night before, the snow was deep and the roads were completely white. Back in Göreme I had spent days playing in the snow and following tracks made by animals, the original roads. Now, all the snow had disappeared and dust had come in its place. Swirling, up your nose, down your throat dust that stuck on Vita's chain; everything was brown; this was to be the colour of the land for the next three months until I reached the Indus.

Dogubeyazit was small, a clandestine place and I immediately felt that I needed to watch my possessions a little more closely. In my diary I wrote that it was a cross between the Wild West and a Dostoyevsky novel. Raskolnikovian characters hid within their greatcoats. In fact, the parting words from the handsome Kurd were, 'Be careful!' I found a little hotel run by two teenage brothers and booked a trip for the next day, my thirty-third birthday. In the hotel I met a young Norwegian, Osmund, who decided to come along too.

No amount of wandering around the town, observing the transitional nature of it and the suspicious looks on many people's faces, could match the experience of the next day with the Kurdish hotel brothers and their cousins.

I woke up, sang happy birthday to myself, ate a chocolate orange that I had saved and went out into the street. There, slouched in the dust, was a low-slung, twenty-seven-year-old sedan, a Toyota I think, with what looked like twenty-seven-year-old tyres on it. The tyres were to be the least of our worries.

I got into the back, lady-like style and squeezed in next to Osmund and two Kurds (more cousins). It was ridiculously uncomfortable. Zafar, the driver, had his brother ride shotgun. Their seats were set so low the young men could hardly see out the window, but at least they looked cool. James Dean, Kurdish style.

Off we went. It was a perfect, blue-skied, warm day. Our first stop was the black market petrol station, which was actually a man standing on the dusty (natch) street corner with a watering can full of petrol. Petrol was smuggled over the border from Iran and was about a tenth of the official price. Nicely filled up 'just in case', but without the windscreen cleaned, we headed down the road towards Iran. I had asked Zafar to take us to three places: a meteor site, somewhere where we could see Mt Ararat and the supposed site of Noah's Ark.

It's apparently harder to get to the crater now as it's so close to the border, but Zafar bumped and scraped us there with ease. I would love to say massively enthusiastic things about the crater, which will make you want to visit it yourself, but, um, it was a big hole in the ground. That's about it for me, a non-geologist. I think the journeys to these places are often more worthwhile than what you see when you get there, and boy were we having fun. Zafar had loaded up the tape deck with Turkish music and the galloping rhythms immediately picked you up and lifted you into a fun palace.

And then the engine cut out.

This was clearly the 'case' in the phrase 'just in case'. Zafar seemed completely unperturbed. He admitted that the car had a hole, just a small one mind you, in the petrol tank, so no problem, he could just nip back to the friendly man on the dusty corner and get some more petrol. He waved down a car and said he would be back very soon. We waited on the side of the road, me thinking that we would never see him again and the boys/men swinging themselves to and fro on an old sign. Zafar came back swinging a petrol can and off we went again.

Now it was time to find the Ark, or the geological aberration that was believed to be the Ark. This site, discovered by a Turkish Army Captain called Durupinar, has pretty conclusively been dismissed as being the Ark (should we talk about whether the Ark even existed?), but it was still fascinating to see what all the fuss might have been about. We turned south off the main road and headed up the mountainside, all muddy from the recent thaw. We skidded and slid, the ancient tyres now having to admit they were more like racing slicks than sturdy mud grippers. Zafar said we had to get out and push. After ten minutes or so of shoving the car up the mountainside, Osmund noticed there were some tyre chains in the back. How very helpful. With the Norwegian chain expert at hand, they were put on quicker than I have ever seen since and we all piled back into the car. So, enough petrol, chains on the tyres, what could go wrong?

Zafar was one of those very enthusiastic drivers who love to rev the engine, as it really is the answer to any problem, driving included. Especially if you are a teenage boy. He revved it and revved it, and revved it a little more. We inched up the steep river of mud and then the car said no and the gearbox started pouring out smoke. At first I thought that Zafar was having a fag to make him even more relaxed. He looked at the smoke, turned to me and grinned and said, 'Don't worry. We'll be going downhill soon.'

That car is probably still going. In fact, that car probably *is* the Ark.

We finally made it to Noah's place, not quite two by two, and walked around the supposed bow and stern and looked across the sea of dust and road to Mt Ararat. The belief that this really was the Ark was very strong for many years. The size, according to many people and the Bible, was right, there were even stones in the area that looked like the anchor stones of the time, but it seems like it was only ever mud. And the stones were for a pagan, not a nautical, purpose. We threw snowballs at each other and headed for the valley and Dogubeyazit again. Once back on the main road, guess what? We ran out of petrol. Zafar and his brother headed off this time and we were left, a band of brothers it seemed now, by the side of the road once more.

Thinking back on this, after all these years, the thing that strikes me most about this day is how safe I felt. Never, not once, was I worried that all these young men would take us off somewhere and rob us, and more. We delighted in them, and they delighted in us. In the evening they invited us to a restaurant overlooking the Pasha's palace (I was the only woman) and we danced Kurdish style, arm in arm, moving only shoulders and legs. And then, the final gift from the Kurds, a birthday cake. It remains my best birthday.

Turkish Dogubeyazit then, was porous and alive with Iranian petrol, Iranian foodstuffs, Kurdish culture, and Iranian and Kurdish and Turkish people. People here were the same as the people over the border. The town was no longer quite Turkish or Kurdish, but it wasn't quite Iranian either.

I went shopping to buy clothes that would turn me into an acceptably dressed woman in the eyes of Muslims. Cycling was barely acceptable in Iran — in fact girls over the age of seven were forbidden to cycle — but I hoped that if my legs were covered by a long coat the religious police would turn a blind eye.

What I had begun to appreciate on my trip was that most people thought I was a man. I had my hair short and, really, what woman travels on her own through such places? It is fascinating what people tell themselves to expect and what that makes them not see. My problem now was that I was going to have to dress clearly as a woman; there would be no 'border dwelling' of my own. I bought a long, flared blue coat and a headscarf. I entered the shop as a scruffy indeterminately gendered Westerner and came out a strict Islamic Republic of Iran-approved lady.

The first time I was made aware I didn't really look like a girl, I was about ten. I used to go swimming a lot in the summer, and one time I was entering the girls' changing rooms and a snippy woman said I was going the wrong way. This comment has echoed through my life. At the Lincoln Center in New York, women in fur coats looked up to check they were going into the correct bathrooms as I exited. Asian women shrieked as I went to the bathroom in hotels in Hong Kong. I steel myself now and accept that I am a border dweller in the world of gender, neither feeling, nor indeed wanting to feel, particularly male or female. I do admire people who are by birth penumbral but have the courage and desire to be firmly one or the other and go through a sex change, but I like the fluidity of being able to float around the middle; I really do think that the basic this or that of male and female is shallow and limiting. How simplistic to think, with all those opposing hormones flowing in each of our bodies, that we are one and therefore not the other. And how much better in countries like India and Thailand that they recognise more than two sexes. More variations in the octave, more variations in gender.

So when I donned the headscarf, I was annoyed at being shoved firmly into the female corner. (In Kabul I met an Australian female diplomat who simply refused to wear the headscarf, but that seemed to be remarkably rude, even for a diplomat.)

The viola is the perfect instrument for someone like me, a musical demonstration of being between commonly known things. When I tell people I play the viola, they often ask if it is like a violin or a cello. It's a big violin, it's a small cello, it's a perfectly sized viola. The viola is rarely appreciated for itself; it often plays the supporting role or the inner part. But without the viola, quartets and orchestral pieces would sound a little hollow and empty.

* * *

Despite thinking the viola was perfect for my gender identity, I was still struggling with whether I should take up the cello or not. I began to apply the same thought process I had used when I decided to do my bike trip. I asked my ninety-year-old self, who refused to answer quickly, and I also remembered the Brahms Trio in B Major.

I studied viola for a postgraduate year in West Berlin in 1988–89. I had lessons with Bruno Giuranna, who was considered one of the finest players and teachers at the time and clearly knew it, with his monogrammed cuffs and dictatorial manner. Lessons were every month, masterclass-style, so there was a lot of time to explore the city (by bicycle), and still do eight hours' practice a day. I lived in a little flat, in the Hinter-Hinterhof, or inner courtyard, of a block in the working-class district of Moabit. Most of the blocks of flats had been built during Berlin's great expansion in the early 1900s and, like most, mine had one room and no bathroom. I sub-let it from an artist and heated it during the minus-ten-degrees-inside winters with an enormous built-in coal oven. Autumn began to get seriously cold as soon as I moved there in October and Hannah the artist gave me instructions on how to light the fire: go down to the coal cellar, get a box of coal, carry it up four steep flights of stairs, stack the bricks just so in the grate, roll up newspaper, light it and da-dah, a warming, toasty fire.

No such thing. I was there, on my knees for three hours trying to get that bloody thing lit. I had no choice. It was certainly character building for a twenty-one-year-old.

Between the fire lighting, the practice and the sightseeing, I also made friends with another viola player called Sophie who invited me around to her (warm) apartment. One morning she was playing a record, a Sony LP of Dame Myra Hess, Isaac Stern and Pablo Casals playing Brahms, his Trio in B major.

Piano trios are tricky beasts. The three players need to be soloistic, more so than in quartets, yet conjoined at the same time. The way many piano trios are written, the melody is thrown around the three parts equally and you need to be able to grab that moment of the limelight like a great diva, then support with the humility of a chorus member. Brahms wrote four piano trios and only three string quartets. He admitted to having written and then destroyed twenty quartets before he allowed one to be published. Brahms stood on the shoulders of the giant Beethoven and sometimes that height gave him vertigo, hence the destruction of so much music; at other times the honour of being named the next great composer gave him the confidence to be able to write grand, weighty symphonies and piano concertos. Beethoven hardly ventured into the key of B major, his adventures were in other directions, but Brahms, even as a young man, was game to go to this new, relatively unexplored land. B major is a reasonably unusual key. B minor, which is the relative minor of D major with just two sharps, is more common, but B major with those five sharps is not at the forefront of most composers' harmonic arsenals. In fact when you say B for German-speaking musicians, they use it for B flat. If they want to say B natural, neither sharp nor flat, they say H. Go figure. Brahms' music often is played in a rather heavy, lugubrious way, but with this piece it's difficult to make it heavy, it is so full of lightness of being.

Much of classical music changes key, or modulates, part way through. This is to bring new colours into the sound. In pop music song structure there is a verse, then there's a chorus, repeat two or three times, then there will be a bridge section, for instance a solo for guitar or saxophone, then the chorus returns. This is often extremely satisfactory, but the music will usually stay in the same key. There might be a key change for dramatic effect at the very end, especially if it is a song performed on *Eurovision* or *The Voice*. In classical music from the Renaissance through to, well, now, really, music begins in a certain key for the first subject, or main tune, then will usually travel clockwise to the next key round the circle of fifths (called the relative fifth) for the second subject. Then, if the composer wants to go to a different place again, they might go to the major/minor key that shares the key signature, for example C major/A minor; B flat major/G minor. You could imagine it like a baseball field. The home plate is the tonic key, first base is the relative fifth, second base is the relative major/minor, third base is a return to the relative fifth via possibly another key, and then you go back to home plate for the end and the return to the tonic. So if you start in B major, as Brahms decided to, the relative fifth (add a sharp) is F sharp major and the relative minor is G sharp minor. All of these keys are in a fairly far-flung harmonic land, so actually it's not surprising that Brahms also uses B minor (not so far-flung) for two of the four movements.

B major on a string instrument has a particularly ethereal sound, as few of the open strings of the instrument vibrate sympathetically any more. The E string alone remains, but gone are the supportive, backing band vibrations of the C, G, D and A strings. Playing in B major means you have to re-map your fingerboard and put fingers in places where once were dragons. A first finger goes on an A sharp, a second on a B, where normally a first would go. It is a key to wrong-foot you. To wrong-finger you.

When the cello melody sang out that Sunday morning in Berlin, reclining on the bed of B major-ness of the piano, I was charged back in time to when I was eight, sitting at home listening to Jacqueline du Pré play Elgar. There was a sincerity and an outwardness to the music, a view of something other, something higher and better, that I had never really captured in my viola playing. Well, I was listening to one of the all-time greats of the cello, so the sound of the cello once again captured something in my soul; I mourned the day my mum put me down for the violin.

Still, I stuck to the viola and I practised and practised, then practised more until each day I had done the requisite eight hours. Playing the viola felt like kneading dough: you needed to work away at it until it was soft and pliable. Until *I* was soft and pliable. I kept this amount of practice up for two months then realised I was spiralling into an obsessive depression, so backed off to four hours a day; my playing improved much more quickly.

My poor German neighbours. In the summer, with the double-insulation windows thrown open, they would shout at me to shut up. Fair enough, unless you loved minimalist music. The first hour was taken up with slow bows on each of the four strings, very loud through to very quiet; crescendos and diminuendos from the tip of the bow to the frog and back again. The next few hours were variations of bowing and string-crossing exercises: spiccato, sautillé, legato, détaché, jeté, martelé. Finally, in hours seven and eight, I got to play notes other than the four open strings by adding some left-hand exercises.

The four strings can be remarkably satisfying, even if you are six years old. One of my little beginner students, Chloë, has been playing open strings to make sure her bowing is secure; one day I announced with great fanfare that it was time for her to use her other hand to make different notes on the fingerboard.

'Really, are there more notes than these?' Chloë's big eyes took in a wider glimpse of the universe of music.

Practising that much and that devotedly really made a huge difference to my playing. When I returned to England and played again with my quartet, they gave me the ultimate accolade of that time and our world. 'Wow, you sound like a teacher.'

B for Berlin, B for B major. My flat was an eyrie, a B major eyrie; I lived alone, I hardly saw people apart from Sophie, I was apart from the world for that year. I was poor, just poor enough, and I loved the solitude and the permission to be completely selfish. Then summer came; I no longer had to struggle with the coal oven and with the summer came the thrill of a meeting in East Berlin with the Škampa Quartet.

My quartet had gone to Prague in 1988 on a musical exchange with the Prague Conservatory. We had gone there and the Škampa Quartet had come to Manchester. This was my first trip to a Communist country, although I had been there many times in books and music: Solzhenitsyn, Shostakovich, Milan Kundera. We travelled with Chris Rowland, our chamber music coach. Chris pointed out suspicious radios in the rooms we were staying in at the conservatory and wondered why we couldn't manage to get any sound from them. I realise now he was winding us up. We met the Škampa Quartet after our concert at the Dvorak hall and they whisked us off to a disco in their Škoda. We fell in love with their brilliance, their humour, their otherness of living behind the Iron Curtain. We loved their pure concentration on music, not distracted by flippant things like fashion and capitalism and too many marmalade choices. We all met again at a music course with the Takács Quartet in the Netherlands, where we had to help them push-start their Škoda; when I moved to West Berlin they suggested we meet up in East Berlin for a day. This was in the summer of 1989, a few months before the fall of the Iron Curtain and only a few weeks before the Hungarians made the first cracks in it, although we had no idea what was about to happen. Cath and Miranda came to stay and we crossed the border at Checkpoint Charlie. I had brought oranges, as they were hard to buy in the East. The East German guard counted them very carefully and we were allowed through, after changing the requisite amount of money. We had arranged to meet the Škampas in Alexanderplatz, below the big tower. And so, at the appointed time, like a scene from a love story, they appeared out of the early morning mist and we went off for our magical day together. It was a day of B major, of floating above the earth. The kind of day that happens when you are so blissfully focused on your life that nothing else breaks through your B major force field.

B major then, is the key of a distant, alien, yet dreamt-of land, a key of heaven, or nirvana. Playing in B major, you feel as if your feet are no longer on earth. Richard Strauss shows this very clearly in the enormous *Also Sprach Zarathustra*. And where better, one would think, to listen to this than the desert where the eternal flame of Zoroastrianism is still, literally, burning?

Fire took on a new meaning when I moved to Australia. In this country a Pommie bastard (affectionate term?) quickly comes to the realisation that life is not secure, no matter the season. In England the only things you die from are old age and bad food, but here there is always an insect, reptile or cataclysmic weather pattern lurking around the next gum tree and you'd better make the most of the time you have left — that is, ten seconds before a brown snake/funnelweb spider combo bites your pale ankles then beats you at cricket.

When I first came to Sydney in December 2001, it was a time when fire seemed to surround the city and lay siege to any lingering ideal of a safe suburban life.

Fire was everywhere. Fire was over the hill, glowing at night-time on the Central Coast; fire in our noses, fire on our skin, remnants on stubborn trees and fire waiting for the sun to come to a broken bottle in the forest. A north wind quickly became an evil thing, accompanied by its own brass section of shrill trumpets and shattered trombones. It was impossible in those times to remember that fire is also sacred, useful and, fingers crossed, controllable.

As a child I'd been obsessed by fire in that completely overwhelming way that children have. I would have a nightly ritual of arranging various stuffed animals, including Badger from *Wind in the Willows*, in the same precise way. Obviously if this did not happen for any reason I would burn to death just like the fireman who visited our primary school said I might. Recently a friend pointed out that rusting is a (very) slow fire. I wish I had known that when I was six. It makes fire seem much kinder. Or rusting scarier.

In the middle of the desert in Iran, fire is a sacred symbol for the Zoroastrians. Zoroaster had two meanings for me before cycling across Iran — the mark of Zorro (natch) and *Also Sprach Zarathustra*, the Strauss tone poem, known by some as a tome poem. Surrounded by the austere landscape of central Iran, Strauss' music seemed overwrought, fickle and a little bit silly. Only the beginning — where the bass, contra bassoon and organ play the low C, then the brass play those three optimistic notes, C, go up five notes to G, go up four notes to C an octave higher — seemed to demonstrate the austerity of the land. The music immediately turns to confusion with the major third depressed to the minor third. And then the thunderous, pompous timpani, with their march of self-importance, take the music off to irrelevant ports for this place. For this desert. At the end, though, Strauss captures the etherealness of the desert with a B major chord, mixed with a C major chord. A clash or a merging of earth and heaven.

Yazd in the noughties, and I mean the beginning of the first century noughties, was a major city for Zoroastrianism and still has a fire temple on the outskirts where a flame has been burning continuously for over 1500 years. When I visited, the flame was being watched like a hawk by the temple guardian, a gnome-like distillation of a man, ageless, wordless, with slightly charred fingers. Flying around the mountains in the area were eagles and vultures, although the Towers of Silence where the Zoroastrians laid their dead are now unused.

A young man from a chicken shop took me to the towers one day. I'd been to get some bread from the bakers, something you need to do three times a day as the bread is thin and stays fresh for exactly twenty-seven minutes. After a few hours — that is, from breakfast to lunchtime — you would need to soak any leftover bread in water to eat it, but that problem is solved when you are cycling and can eat a whole round in one meal; so off I went to buy more bread and there, waiting in line at the hot counter beside the oven where bread was clinging to the walls, was a thin, refined young chap with a briefcase who spoke clear, simple English. He was on the cusp of manhood. This meant that he still had the curiosity of childhood and not yet the reserve of Muslim male adulthood; he politely asked me if I would like him to take me to the Towers of Silence. In retrospect, it was such a beautiful question; it seemed to hold the promise of a place beyond the here and now. In reality it meant that he would borrow his dad's Hillman Hunter and drive me to the towers on the outskirts of the city.

I was surprised to see Hillmans when I arrived in Iran. Gran'ma had had a golden one and seeing this mass of Hillman

Hunters made me think of thousands of Gran'mas, all delivering meals on wheels and taking young girls to cycling euphoria.

Hamid, my Towers of Silence guide, stated quite boldly that women are the same as men, but that in the Iranian culture they always seemed to be beneath men. He seemed disappointed in this, but accepted there was nothing he could do. He didn't want to marry until he was forty and said that it was his duty to take me around. He left me at lunchtime, so I thought that was the end of our time together. I spent the afternoon reading and saw Hamid the next day.

'Where did you go?'

He looked hurt and said that he had been waiting for me. It turned out that he couldn't afford to pay for both of us at lunch so he had left me at the restaurant; he wanted to continue the tour in the afternoon and had gone looking for me.

Such endless hospitality, such impossible to imagine kindness: free bread; invitations to people's homes; a visit to Persian rock musicians who had just done an underground gig in Tehran; a woman coming up to me in her chador revealing only her face, calling me 'darling' and talking of the delights of being a drama student in Bournemouth; Akbar, opening the gate to his guesthouse in Bam with the surprise claim, 'I've been expecting you.' And his son Mohammed who modestly stated, 'I'm a chip off the old block.'

Iranian society seemed curiously upside down, with the older generation the ones who had travelled, who spoke English and had heard Western sixties pop music and had grown up with a looser moral compass. The young ones in Iran had much tighter controls on their life by the State. Akbar told me they still had sex before marriage, though, they just did it anally.

I was in Iran for six weeks. My visa was originally for a month, but a lovely official happily extended it. I didn't quite give him the full story on why I was travelling so slowly; I mumbled something about how much I loved the country, not how I could only cycle one hundred and fifty kilometres a day. I was in a strange in-between place with cycling in Iran; it was illegal for locals so barely legal for me. As I went further south I was more aware of people's disapproval: shocked stares from cars, fewer shouts of 'Hello lady', so I did the very simple and very illegal thing of taking off my headscarf. By this time I had lost so much weight that I hardly had any chest and was cycling in a long shirt that an Afghan tailor had made for me in Yazd; the temperature was rising, high twenties in the middle of the day, and I couldn't stand the restrictiveness of my blue coat from Dogubeyazit. As soon as I threw off that headscarf and coat and crossed the gender border, all my troubles went away and I made it to the Iranian border with Pakistan.

Crossing the border from Zahedan to Taftan was not without its Pythonesque challenges. My American-made, aluminium-framed, twenty-one gear Cannondale bicycle and I rolled up to the first Iranian Customs desk, walking my bike and preparing to declare nothing. Things I should have declared: partying in Tehran, advising students which schools to go to in the West, comparing muscles with young women, being offered champagne and declining it, having sex out of wedlock, oh and cycling a few thousand kilometres across their country. As I had decided to declare none of these things, I was excited to soon be leaving and going somewhere new, somewhere with different challenges and obviously, a completely different landscape because it would be a completely different country fifty metres over there, right?

It was now time for the second Iranian Customs desk, five minutes walk away across a very dusty courtyard. When you see two Customs desks, it's time to get worried.

'Where is your carnet de passage for the bike?'

I thought the Customs officer was joking and I did in fact laugh. I mean, that's a good joke. If anything needed and indeed deserved its own paperwork, it was my bike, Vita. She is downstairs right now, a bit chipped in the top tube, but still elegant and a joy to ride. At this point in the trip I had had no punctures and no mechanical problems whatsoever. If I could, I would kiss the feet of Mr Jones the bike mechanic and Mr Cannondale. If you are reading this, Mr Cannondale, don't feel like you need to send me a new bike to thank me for free advertising because my old one will see me through, you made her so well. Maybe send one to the Iranian restaurant painters instead.

My bike didn't need a carnet de passage, she needed a medal ceremony.

Anyhow, back to the joke, which was not a joke. This was turning into a 'situation'. I admitted I had no carnet, but also pointed out, in as unsnotty a way as I could, that I didn't need one. I had entered Iran without needing one, and surely the same rules applied from one side of the country to the other? Apparently not. I was dismissed, with the words, 'Bring us your carnet de passage.'

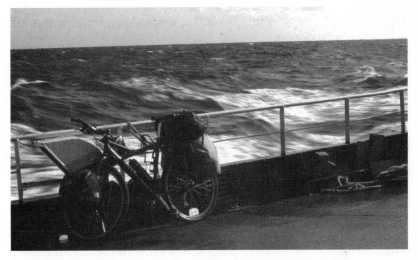

One of my favourite portraits of Vita. Named after Vita Sackville-West, because of her unusual shape and very, very strong character.

They might as well have asked me to play the Tchaikovsky Violin Concerto from memory. In that short a time frame, it just wasn't going to happen.

I went back to the first Customs officer and asked if he could give me a carnet for my bike.

'You don't need a carnet for your bike.'

ARGHH. This back and forth went on for half an hour, with slightly different words each time, but each time edging closer to everybody losing their patience. It was a game of boredom in the end. The second Customs officer, after watching me cycle (I'd given up politely walking) back and forth between the two posts, finally gave up and let me through, with a sneaky look that made me think he had been winding me up all along.

I entered the final building, officially left the country at Immigration, pulled my headscarf off and walked down a long, dingy corridor. At the end, just inside Iran, was a Pakistani man dressed in shalwar kameez and mirrored hat. He pushed open the creaky iron door, let in a blast of light and said:

'This way, please.'

I lifted Vita over the threshold, as if we were on our honeymoon, and my brain exploded with a burst of colour. There, within a few metres of the border, was a wild and frenzied cricket match.

In all the borders I have crossed, I have never seen two such different sides as Pakistan and Iran. Not even Pakistan and India. Despite them sitting on the same plateau with the same desert, I had gone from the seriousness and dour tones of Iran and stepped through a magic gate into a gorgeous painting. I walked around the cricketers, freewheeled over to the Immigration building, low-set and British-looking, and steered my bike into the office. A short, twinkly eyed man sat at a desk eating his lunch — paratha and daal.

'Madam, would you like it if I wheeled my car into your living room?'

I admitted that it probably would make the carpet a bit grubby.

'Then please, would you do me the good favour of leaving your mode of transport outside?

'And would you like some tea?'

I had finally arrived in the country whose embassy officials had laughed me out of the room. I was in Pakistan and I loved it already.

F sharp major/minor/
G flat major/minor

Six sharps, six flats. With enharmonic keys, their combined accidentals always add up to twelve. Accidentals — sharps, flats, naturals, tooth mishaps.

The tea I was given was milky and gloriously spicy. That small cup of chai is now forever in my mind the perfect cup of tea, like a Plato blueprint. It arrived on a tray, direct from tea heaven. I was so surprised to see and smell and taste milky tea after drinking black tea across Turkey and Iran, I must have appeared somehow displeased.

The Immigration officer eyed me as I sipped at the little glass. 'You don't like our tea?'

'You have no idea how much I love this tea.'

Despite feeling welcomed by Iranians across their country, I have to admit to feeling a slight relief about leaving it. There was an occasional heaviness, desperation even, to some people's interactions with me. After six weeks, I was utterly exhausted.

This may sound mean and I'm sorry if it does. Back in 2000 very few Westerners were travelling to Iran so sometimes it felt as if I were doing public relations for everybody. Perhaps the most remarkable time, in fact a week when I ended up having to keep an appointments diary (who needs one of those when they are travelling?), was in Tehran.

I arrived in Tehran in February 2000. After getting stuck on a motorway (again) I found my way to the Azadi Square and Tower, the symbol of Tehran and scene of many of the Revolution demonstrations, and made my way downtown. It really is amazing to now, at my fingertips, be able to look on the Internet at the very route I took through Tehran.

I joined the roiling sea of Hillman Hunters wending their way east into town, the light dropping low in the sky behind us. My hotel was some way away so I took it easy, trying to blend in (unlikely) and allowing myself to be amazed by this experience. Overseas news that had managed to filter through to my childhood mind had all been about Iran: the Shah, the Ayatollah, the Revolution, the hostages and the Iran–Iraq War; so to be here, cycling, was almost incredible for me. A bit like cycling into an intense childhood novel.

I got stuck behind a bus in the traffic. The buses throughout Iran are segregated, with women at the back and their own separate entrance. I did wonder why anyone bothered, as people in taxis seemed to be stuffed in any old how. The bus stopped frequently and I bided my time, observing and being observed. I eventually noticed two girls who were giggling and staring at me from the back seat. I waved at them and they pulled their chadors over their faces. This cat and mouse, hare and tortoise game continued for most of the main street. It was the equivalent of cycling down George Street in Sydney, or Oxford Street in London. Finally the two girls got off the bus. I smiled at them and they dallied in the gloaming, waiting for me to speak.

'Do you speak English?'

'Yes. We are going to our English lesson.'

You know show and tell, where you are asked to bring an item to school to display and talk about it? Well, I was their show and tell that evening. They asked if I would like to join them, so I pushed my bike alongside them through the end-of-day crowds, brushing past endless chadors and men with tight trousers and immaculately coiffed hair, making our way to their English lesson in the middle of Tehran. It turned out that the two girls were Jewish, some of the few remaining Jews in the country, and that they were waiting on their visa to emigrate to Israel. Their names were Elham and Edna. I forgot to ask them what grade they got for that lesson.

This was the beginning of a whirlwind of social engagements in Tehran. Everywhere I went young people wanted to talk to me and arrange to have tea so they could quiz me on life in the West. A young man called Adeen, who played the tar (a type of lute), wanted help with studying in the States. Teachers from the

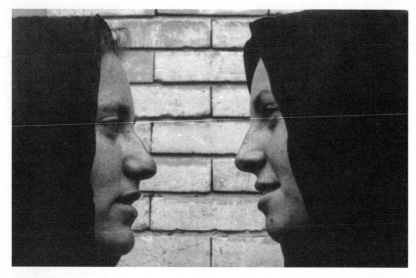

English-language students in Tehran. I've never had so much fun ramming a snowball down inside someone's chador.

English school invited me to their homes and showed me their depilatory methods. The students took me skiing in the mountains, up in a cable car, throwing snowballs and experimenting with how far back they could wear their headscarfs, or hijab, before they were pulled over by the religious police. The girls had to be modest, and the boys did too, but they wore tighter clothes than the girls, despite no body shape-revealing clothes being allowed. This law was flouted at every turn. So was the one about not being materialistic. Shabnam, an English teacher, stated very boldly that the religious laws were simply a way to suppress the population and that people would always do what they wanted. She said that Iranians were in fact not particularly religious people and that materialism was very strong. One night we went to a party; everybody had their chadors off, the host changed her clothes twice and people were so surprised to see my muscles that they came and squeezed them. Because these women did no manual work and were steered away from exercising by their culture, they had bodies similar perhaps to the Western aristocracy of the 1700s.

I left the social whirl of Tehran (what a very surprising phrase that is) and moved on to Qom. Here it was quite the opposite. I somehow felt not exactly unwelcome, but it seemed a little rude to be there and I took great care to leave as early in the morning as I could, walking my bike to beyond the city limits.

In a particularly keen attempt in another town to have me stay, one hotel manager told me the hotel was full, then insisted I go to his house. This was extremely generous and had even happened before, in the north; one hotel guy had invited me to his flat instead and I ended up having a great time with him and his wife, who used to swim when she was younger and now smoked instead.

I was touched, although reluctant, to go to the manager's house, as I also just wanted to zone out and not talk to anybody for a night. I had no option and tried to be gracious in accepting. We walked over to his house, me thinking that I would be quite safe as so many people had seen us together and it was quite a small town. I ended up having a blast, playing Bach as he accompanied me on the tabla. I asked him if he was married; he said yes and that his wife would be home soon. All evening he kept repeating that his wife would be home soon. In the end it got to about eleven o'clock and there was no sign of his wife. Hotel man rolled out two beds in the same room and said we should go to sleep. I did go to bed, but did not sleep one single wink. His foot kept touching mine and it was all I could do to not totally freak out and panic. Of course his intentions were honourable, but as another traveller pointed out, it is very unusual for a Muslim man to not know where his wife is.

Now I was in Pakistan, I was also looking forward to cycling in a country where I might be hassled less. I hate to say bad things about Iran, because God knows enough people bag the country, but there were a few instances where my leg was grabbed by boys on scooters and there were endless shouts of 'Phwoaar', or at least the Farsi equivalent. This happened everywhere, not just Iran, but there was an edge to it in the south of the country that was beginning to bother me. So much so that I had caught a bus for the final hundred kilometres to the border. As I travelled further south, the country became wilder and the towns poorer. One of the most alarming events was when I was leaving Kerman. It was a Saturday and there was hardly any traffic on the road. I was going along at a pretty good clip; most of the time I would cycle at about twenty-five kilometres an hour; if the wind was behind me, that could rise to forty. One time I met a Japanese guy coming the opposite way. I had had the wind behind me for a week and he had had to struggle with the wind in his face, doing fourteen kilometres an hour. He looked completely worn out.

So I was pedalling away, a nice light cadence, and heard a car pull up behind me. This often happened; I would wave at them, they would wave at me, drive past slowly and stare, then go ahead. Sometimes I would see them again waiting at the side of the road. They would flag me down and ask for a photo and we would all go away thinking how lovely we all were.

This time was different. It was a single man. He drove beside me and didn't say anything; he simply stared. I said hello, trying to be polite, and kept cycling. He went in front of me and slowed down, then came back beside me and stared again. I began to get scared. It was such a quiet day and I had not seen any other cars all morning. My only defence was a spray can of mace and a pretty good left hook. I stopped cycling, stood astride Vita in what I hoped was a truly menacing way and waited for him to drive on. He didn't. I got back on Vita and stupidly tried to pedal away as fast as I could. He and his two-litre engine caught up with me. I stopped again, got out my mace and shouted at him. He pulled his car across my path. I picked up some stones and threw them at him.

At this moment, this terrifying moment, which every woman dreads will happen to them, another car came up behind us. Once again, a single man. Oh no, they are working as a team. This new guy challenged the first one, spoke harshly to him and they both drove away. I stood there shaking, the mace in my hand, my legs barely able to hold me up. I pulled over to the side of the road and burst into tears.

There were moments on this monumental journey when I felt strangely at home in foreign lands, but also moments when I felt very, very far from home. The sense of key, the sense of the journey between Hong Kong and England, seemed weaker in these moments and I felt anchorless and directionless. I always did have a direction, though (east), and I was grateful for that. I met so many people who were travelling with no particular purpose.

The sense of a key in music is unquestionably vital. Time and time again I have heard people say:

'Oh I've got nothing against modern music, but it just leaves me cold. I mean, where's the tune?'

By tune, I think many people mean, 'Where's the sense of key?'

It's true there is a lot of music that doesn't have a memorable tune. Some of the hits of the eighties spring to mind, but I have to admit that there is not one piece by Schoenberg for instance, which I could instantly whistle. There is something about that comfort of the tonic, of the home note, that satisfies our human longing. The tonic is a log fire, it's your children laughing at the window, it's familiar public transport and the smell of your favourite dish cooking. The tonic is belonging. When composers take you away from the tonic, it is with the understanding that no matter how far they take you from it, they will always, ALWAYS, bring you back. Try to imagine a Beethoven symphony ending on the penultimate chord and you will immediately know what that means.

When Schoenberg, Berg and Webern started to break down the long-established rules of harmony in the early 1900s, it is no surprise that people baulked. Schoenberg introduced a method of composing called serialism, where you use the twelve semitones of the octave equally. One way to think of it is by considering one of the most famous sentences ever written and swapping notes for words:

'All animals are created equal, but some are more equal than others.'

In Schoenberg's new compositional method, this series is called a tone row and from the basic statement, he manipulated it as extensively and thoroughly as his imagination would let him. The only rule was that every note had to be used each time. So you might have:

'Others than equal more are some but equal created are animals all.'

Or:

'All are animals created equal some but are more than equal others.'

This would happen in one line of the piece, but would also be happening in the harmony as well.

I'm sure you can get an app for it nowadays.

Composers before Schoenberg et al. had pushed open the envelope of harmony, but they still had some familiar rules, some harmonic decency. Even Stravinsky and the *Rite of Spring* had moments of tonality, moments of you feeling like you had come home. Still, it is incredible to think that harmony and its variations can cause riots, as happened at the *Rite of Spring*'s first performance in 1913. When Berg wrote his opera *Wozzeck* in 1917, it was the first use of atonality in an opera and it caused an enormous storm, even though Berg was able to live off the opera's royalties for a while. Hitler put a stop to performances, declaring the music decadent. Hitler knew what people wanted, just like Madame Mao and Stalin did. They wanted tonality.

Harmony, and the power of a chord, goes to the very heart of our emotions.

Very early Western harmony started in the ninth century with something called 'organum'. It is incredibly simple — a melody, with one other part moving in the same way and simply a fifth apart. Up to the 1300s, certain intervals, or distances between two notes were banned. Unison notes were all right, as were fourths and fifths and octaves; these are perfect intervals and sound relatively open. They are neither major nor minor. Think of Chinese music as well; that is mostly made up of fifths.

The inclusion of thirds and sixths in a piece was tantamount to heresy. These intervals were seen as being too manipulative, too emotional. If you think of their use in pop music today, you'll hear why. Think the Dixie Chicks or the Righteous Brothers. And the augmented fourth or tritone, well, that was called the devil's third and it would never have been heard unless nature made the sound. Imagine the shower scene in *Psycho* — that is an augmented fourth. You can try these intervals with your vacuum cleaner. When I was a kid I used to practise intervals when Mum was hoovering and it works quite well. Take the vacuum cleaner note as your tonic, then sing up the scale, counting the tonic as one. Sing one note above that and you have a second. One above that and you have a third etc. You can then play around by singing a minor third by dropping a half step, or a devil's third, otherwise known as an augmented fourth, by going up another whole step from the major third.

So harmony is power over your emotions. And the ability for disharmonic harmony to make you feel completely unsettled should not be underestimated.

My student quartet had spent a couple of years studying Haydn, Mozart and Beethoven, the masters of the first Viennese School. The school where the tonic was king. Dr Chris Rowland, our teacher, called us into his studio one day and gave us four identical scores. Four scores each including four parts to a piece by Webern called *Six Bagatelles*. We had graduated to the second Viennese School, where the tonic no longer existed. Monarchy was gone; communism had taken its place. The Webern bagatelles were extremely short, the whole piece about five minutes, but they were so complicated that each player had their own score so that they wouldn't get lost, even in this concise piece.

Actually, concise is a good word to describe Webern's music. Imagine all the emotion of a Mahler symphony, which last around an hour, compressed into a piece a tenth the length. These men were composing around the same time; Mahler died in 1911, the year Webern wrote the bagatelles. Both composers take you to the far-flung limits of human self-awareness, it's just that one does it much quicker. The whole world is in a Mahler symphony, yet here was music that said as much, but with the density of an imploded star. Webern had distilled emotion and made a new and strange elixir.

We left Chris' room feeling a bit shell-shocked. We knew we were about to be given a new piece to learn, but we were thinking maybe Dvorak, late Beethoven. Something we could whistle. We found a practice room, unpacked our instruments and tried to work out how to begin.

Looking at the score to the Webern, it was like poring over an ordnance survey or geoscience map. Where in Mahler a phrase would take several bars, in the Webern an emotion was summed up in a gesture of a very few notes. The amount of detail he managed to squeeze into this short piece was staggering. We started at the beginning. Bar by bar. Each one had so much information in it: crescendos, rallentandos, accents, dynamics, bow markings, articulation, with or without mutes, and nearly every bar a slightly different tempo. After an hour we had made it to maybe bar three. This was going to be a very long trip.

We spent our holidays practising the Webern, until by the end we could play it from memory. To accentuate listening we played in different corners of the room with the lights turned off, all facing away from each other. Gradually the music revealed itself; from an amorphous noise and confusion with no tonic we saw patterns emerge, relationships develop between instruments, arguments flare up and then glorious, if brief, makings-up. Brick by brick we were revealing a new homeland.

The music begins, as the J.S. Bach E Major Prelude does, with a rest. The instruments beckon to you: come! Step into our surreal soundscape! It is Hieronymus Bosch-like, there is as little conformity here as in his art, and the music leaves your heart racing because it is all so intense, so very dense. Like Webern is grabbing hold of your shirt and telling you, 'You must listen to me!' By turns the gestures embrace you then reject you, scold you then love you. It blew our minds. I began to realise that having no key was nothing to be scared about. Who needed a home, when every single note meant so much else?

* * *

I was glad to be in Pakistan, but this border town I had arrived in, Taftan, could not have been more challenging.

There was more dust in that town than I had ever seen before, like all the vacuum cleaners in the whole world had emptied their dustbags in this place. Somebody had been doing a lot of interval singing. There were no women on the streets at all and the lovely Immigration officer, after finishing his lunch, waiting for the other officer to come back from his lunch, finding the key to the cupboard where the rubber stamps were kept and stamping me into the country, told me to be careful.

Many people had advised me not to cycle this part of the journey. The hotel manager in Kerman, after being very appreciative of my Bach C major slow movement, told me it was too dangerous. Policemen said it was too dangerous. Crikey, even drug smugglers themselves would have told me it was too dangerous. The danger was, indeed, drug smuggling. This part of the world has, or did have, a very porous border, including north to Afghanistan; now there is a ten-foot-high wall being built all the way between Iran and Pakistan. The Balochi people indigenous to the area happily straddled the political lines for centuries before the wall was built, but unfortunately so did nefarious drug runners. So it was not hard for me to decide to catch a bus from Taftan to Quetta. The hard thing was finding the bus.

I cycled the dusty road into Taftan, which then was more of a village with lots of chickens, and found the government guesthouse. One good thing left behind by the Brits. I wonder if Pakistani people do the 'What did the Romans ever do for us?' sketch, but with the British?

After leaving my bike and panniers at the suitably grubby guesthouse, I walked back into the village to find out about buses. It was still lunchtime so not many men were standing around, but one guy asked me if I would like to buy a bus ticket to Quetta. I naturally said yes. He invited me into the back of his shop where all his friends were sitting down on cushions eating lunch. They invited me to sit with them and offered me some tea. Nobody said anything to me, yet the silence was somehow companionable. This was my first experience of the art of waiting. I waited for about thirty minutes and then a small piece of paper was given to me in exchange for about $20. Not too much I thought, for a sixteen-hour bus journey. I waved goodbye to my new friends and left. I was told the bus would go past my guesthouse at 6.30 the next morning.

I slept fitfully that night. Being in a new country, hearing all those new sounds, anticipating the new day's events, it all meant that when it was time to get up I was already prepared mentally. I loaded my panniers onto Vita and stood outside, waiting for the bus. At about 6.45am a bus trundled past, slowed as it passed me then trundled on. The same thing happened three more times. Each time I waved and smiled and tried to look like I would be a lovely passenger and that Vita really wouldn't be too much of a hindrance, but each time I was spurned. I began to think I would never be able to leave, or worse, I would have to cycle the dreaded drug-smuggling route. Finally a heaving bus sighed to a stop in front of me. A very, very fat man waved to me from his chaise longue beside the driver.

'Come, come!' he beckoned me. The bus boy from the roof leant down and stuck out an arm for Vita. I quickly pulled off my 'absolutely do not part from this under any circumstances' handlebar bag and lifted Vita up to him. With all her gear on she weighed about thirty kilos and this young boy swept her up in his hand with one smooth motion. I stepped aboard the garishly painted bus and handed over my ticket.

'No no. This is no good. You must buy a ticket. This is not a ticket for this bus.'

I will never know whether I was ripped off, and if so, by whom. Actually I don't really mind. Whoever it was, was so polite about it and they taught me an important lesson. Buy a bus ticket on the bus.

The enormous man waved me aboard after I had parted with another $20, plus $10 for Vita; he made a poor Pakistani man move to the back so that I could have an honoured place at the front, right at his enormous feet. He seemed to be the bus manager and had arranged cushions and pillows for himself beside the driver. He looked after the money, the seating arrangements and people's general welfare for the next sixteen hours to Quetta. He was the bus god and we worshipped him.

I sat next to a young man from Sialkot. Sialkot is a town north of Lahore and is the birthplace of most of the hand-sown footballs in the world. I have no idea what my new friend, Iqbal, was doing in this part of the country, so close to Iran. I thought it best not to ask.

Iqbal was so sweet, he reminded me of the Kurd who gave me half his kebab. He made sure he didn't touch me when I sat

141

down and tried to help by offering to look after my handlebar bag. I politely declined and the driver engaged first gear; the bus gathered all its energy … and rolled forward very slowly. This was going to be a long, wonderful trip.

I was the only woman on the bus. The others were, it seemed, importers, with various plump hessian bags of goodies to be sold in Pakistan. As we headed out of town we all nestled into our positions, always respectful of the bus god. He ignored everybody and cracked nuts continuously.

The little dusty accident of dwellings that was Taftan petered out and the open road beckoned. Up ahead, though, was a roadblock.

The bus shuddered still and the bus god welcomed aboard a Customs officer. Of course. I hadn't cleared Pakistan Customs yet. The shadow of the words 'carnet de passage' darkened my mind. As the only foreigner on board, I had the worrying honour of being invited to disembark and come and join the Customs officer in his hut. I smiled and hoped I would see Vita again in my next life. I sat respectfully as the chap looked through my passport.

Each time I handed over my passport to an official I wished I had got a new, empty passport before I left. My current one was full of interesting-looking visas to places like Vietnam, Russia, Burma, China and, most fascinating of all, the United States of America. This was a working visa for a tour the orchestra had done a few years ago and it had my picture on the visa. Every time an official flipped through my passport, they spent a long time gazing at that page. What was going through their heads? A distant hope of working there themselves, a memory of a cousin who had gone there and never returned, an imagining of life somewhere else other than right here, right now? I sympathised greatly with them; I had been in that place myself, so I smiled and waited. Meanwhile, another Customs officer had boarded the bus and was having an increasingly heated exchange with the bus god. Suddenly the bus engine started up, I mentally said goodbye to Vita and my new friend Iqbal and the bus drove away. The official with me could see the panic in my eyes and very gently said it was all right, they were just going round the corner. He gave me back my passport and sent me away with a sad look.

I followed the bus's tracks to a car park around the back of the Customs hut. There was the bus, slowly being emptied by a little swarm of Customs men, with the now angry bus god looking on. The passengers gathered together and a doctor told me the story. The Customs officials had recently raised the bribe to pass go and collect $200 — just pay the right amount and you could go through Customs without every item being individually searched, and thus save yourself three hours' delay. Our bus god had refused to pay, being an upstanding chap, and the Customs guys were making him pay in another way. We watched as they took everything off. Sacks of spices, bags of rice, legumes, vegetables, schoolbooks, everything apart from Vita. Then the Customs men left, presumably for a cup of tea, and I entertained everybody with some J.S. Bach. After two hours the Customs men sauntered back and ordered us to put everything back on the bus. We were free to go. It had been a battle of waiting and we had won. As we re-embarked, we all paid homage to the bus god with smiles and offers of sweets and bananas.

Off we went, into the Kharan Desert. This place is so remote the Pakistan Army chose it as the testing site for their nuclear weapons. To the south, the Makran Desert had been the undoing of Alexander the Great and his army.

The day slipped slowly by. I looked outside the window at the desert and gazed at the camels lumping past. I napped, feeling quite safe next to Iqbal, and read *Anna Karenina* when I had looked at enough sand. Iqbal asked me where the book was set. I started to launch into a passionate telling of the story: families and trains and teeth and 1800s Russia; Iqbal looked disappointedly at me.

'But you are here!'

How true. How ridiculous to be somewhere so extraordinary, somewhere that I now look at on the map and think, my god, was I really there, and to not actually *be* there. To be in 1800s Russia instead. I closed my book and returned to where I should be. The here and now.

After many hours (our poor bus driver) the bus stopped at a wind- and sand-wrecked shop and we all got out and ate. Parathas, daal. Simple food, eating with our hands. We all snuggled together against the wind, only the bus god remaining on the bus to eat.

Off we set again, further and further into the desert. It was becoming like a minimalist work, with the changes happening so slowly and subtly that you don't recognise they have happened.

Years ago, in the Hong Kong Philharmonic, we had played

I am aged about twelve here,
the year I became a viola player.
Obviously my haircut is modelled
on a Renaissance painting.

Gran'ma. She was about
eighty-eight then, but look at
the fire in those eyes.

In front of Notre Dame, about to leave Paris. Photo by Catherine Rimer — you can hear
her cello-playing on many J.E. Gardiner records. No worries about the plug, Cath.

Brenton being a music stand for his wife, Miranda, who in turn is a music stand for him. Playing duets is tricky.

Local dudes waiting for breakfast in southern Turkey, at the birthplace of St Nicholas in Gelemiş.

The pyjama man in central Iran, with his family. Perfect hosts, kind beyond words. If you're thinking of going to Iran, do it. But maybe take some pyjamas.

The restaurant painters in northern Iran. They looked so guilty when I saw their blue paint on my handlebars, which is only now fading. Iran, home of extra-durable emulsion.

The Friday mosque in Esfahan. The use of water in the inner courtyard made the serenity even more profound.

A Kurd, his car, Mt Ararat. My thirty-third birthday, 2000.

The guardian of the eternal flame of Zoroastrian, just outside Yazd.

Relaxing up in the Karakorams, with one of the Springboks' bikes. Apparently not too hard to relax at about 4000 metres, cycling up a mountain. Very fit, very happy.

A proto-violinist, high up in the Karakorams. This guy couldn't play, yet, but he had a jolly good go and was very reluctant to hand back Aurelia.

The wool sellers of Quetta. They gave me tea, admired my bike and stood so gracefully for this shot. I have this picture up at home and appreciate their tranquillity every day.

The high Karakorams. The sign warning of a bend in the road seems somehow inconsequential in this location. Still, the bend *was* pretty sharp.

Some of the civil servants working at a government guesthouse in the south of Pakistan, just outside Sukkur. These guys wouldn't even let me pay for my board.

Leaving Lahore very early in the morning on my way to India, only about thirty kilometres away.

With a guard at a restaurant in Kabul. You are searched and frisked before you go into any foreigners' restaurant. These guards are so brave and calm, risking their lives just so we can eat in safety.

A woman in Kabul. This image makes me think of the Madonna, the way her hands are seeming to plead under her burqa.

The extraordinary Jini Dinshaw, just before the concert in Mumbai. Jini is very camera-shy, but I think I finally got a pretty good shot of her. And I was lucky enough to sit by her in the concert. Like sitting next to a guru.

The ultimate day: arriving in Hong Kong, 9 December 2000. Photo: K.Y. Cheng/*South China Morning Post*.

Jane and me in southern India. The next day we would survive one hundred kilometres of cycling through tigers, bee stings, Indian traffic and the ubiquitous Indian horn.

Gorecki's *Symphony of Sorrowful Songs*. The work is an enormous lament based on mediaeval chants. It lasts around an hour and is scored also for soprano, who sings the words 'Oh Mamma do not cry — Immaculate Queen of Heaven support me always'.

The words had been scratched into the wall of a Gestapo cell by an eighteen-year-old Polish girl, a prisoner, weeping not for herself, but for her mother. The music builds from a simple phrase in the double basses, a phrase repeated over and over and over again until you cannot help but cry. It has no tonal centre, yet it has many tonal centres. In this music, strangely, everywhere is home.

As each new section enters with the same ancient melody, starting on a different point in the scale, you spin around listening in awe to the simultaneous pain and the comforting. As one voice is in anguish, another brings solace. As one voice cries in dissonance, another responds with consonance. And then, after an epoch of weeping and consolation, the different parts come together on a single note. I thought about us all here on this bus, sitting quietly, looking out into the sand storm surrounding us, moving slowly into the night, sharing the same journey. Coming from such different places, having our own tonal centres, yet giving each other small kindnesses along the way. It made me realise that being at home is a state of mind. So far from any home, I felt a state of bliss.

As the sun was rising, we shambled into Quetta. The same bus driver had driven this entire six hundred and fifty kilometres.

Twenty hours of sand storms, wild trucks, herdsmen, wandering camels and a bus god snoring beside him. As I left the bus I shook his hand and tried to give him a substantial tip. The bus god took it instead.

Quetta is at a crossroads in Asia. It is an enharmonic town. It is only two hundred kilometres from Kandahar in Afghanistan, is often the centre of protracted separatist violence by the Balochis and sits on the route of one of the great strategic passes on the continent: the Bolan Pass. The British had brought twelve thousand troops through the pass in the first Afghan War in 1839 and they eventually did what the British do best, build a railway. To bring a train up to Quetta two special locomotives are needed as the gradient is so severe, one engine pushing and one pulling. A Dr Doolittle machine. When the train descends again to the plain, extra carriages are needed for their braking power alone; to prevent downward trains crashing into stations if their brakes fail, they have to brake fully before the station; if they fail to, they are directed onto a track that goes uphill. The Brits, it seemed, thought of everything. For trains at least.

Quetta is a big city and a very important trade centre; around two million people live there, from many different tribes and backgrounds, hence the continuing violence. As I write this, I have just seen news of a bomb going off in a rickshaw in the city, killing twelve people. There are Muslims and some Christians; ethnically there are Pashtuns, Hazaras, Punjabis, Balochis and a fascinating group called the Brohis. Anthropologists believe they may have come to Quetta through the Bolan Pass from southern India, as they have Dravidian elements to their language; they are the only people to speak a Dravidian-based language outside southern India. And, as the city is so close to Afghanistan, there are many Afghan refugees.

As soon as I stepped off the bus, I felt the sizzle of tension in the place. Riots were commonplace and people recommended I stay in one of the two more upmarket hotels for security. Apparently one of them allowed camping in the grounds, which seemed like a good compromise.

Security is a tricky thing, isn't it? If you surround yourself with too much of it, you shut yourself off from the place you are in, possibly even making yourself more of a target. In Kabul for instance, I was driven around in a Toyota Corolla. Our security consisted of central-locking. Several diplomats from the US and Australia were shocked at this lack of gun power and armouredness, but a Toyota Corolla blends in much better than an armoured four-wheel drive. The same went for Vita. I decided that I would not take a lock for her, as any lock good enough would be far too heavy, and if somebody wanted to steal her, they would be able to cut through any lock I was prepared to lug that far. I told myself that if she were stolen, I would stop my trip. Luckily I didn't have to test that statement.

I went looking for the hotel with the campground.

Vita felt so smooth under me after such a rickety bus journey. By this point, having cycled nearly ten thousand kilometres together, we melded into each other like conjoined twins, or my viola after years of practice. She was fine after being on the top of the bus and had only a new gouge on her top tube. Australian mechanics have often commented that the gouge is worryingly deep, especially for an aluminium-framed bike, but she seems to not be bothered by it. It's her battle scar.

I found the Lourdes Hotel, an institution in Quetta for overland travellers, and cycled up to reception. The hotel manager was in a bad mood that morning and I had to work hard to persuade him to allow me to camp in his grounds. Single female, friendly etc.

'All right. But you can only stay for three nights.'

I ended up staying five. I tucked myself away behind a hedge, hoping he would forget about me, but on the fifth morning the manager marched over and suggested that it was time I went and enjoyed the rest of what Pakistan had to offer.

One thing I was very keen to do in Quetta was visit the Command and Staff College. Field Marshal Montgomery had

A military policeman in the hotel grounds in Quetta. The military in Pakistan were without exception kind, gracious and overwhelmingly helpful.

taught here in the 1930s when he was a colonel, and Thomas Blamey, the only Australian to be awarded the rank of field marshal, had attended the college in 1912. Gran'ma had given me a love of Montgomery. She talked about him a lot when she reminisced about the war. After telling the story of keeping a suitcase of individually wrapped eggs on her lap on the train from Devon to London, an extra sparkle would enter her eye as she repeated Montgomery's speech to the Eighth Army before El Alamein:

'We will stand and fight here! If we can't stay here alive, then let us stay here dead.'

I loved that abruptness with Gran'ma. No pussy footing around, you were either making sense, like Montgomery, or needing a good talking to, like Rommel.

The next morning I awoke to the sound of birdcalls and the muezzin's call to prayer. The various muezzins were all starting at slightly different times and it became an electric fugue of devotion.

After going into town and buying a shalwar kameez, I cycled up to the Staff College. I had attempted to make myself at least a little smart, but frankly I was having trouble. My hair was permanently sticky yet simultaneously dusty, and my skin had taken on the outdoor look of sailors and homeless people. And now, as it was clear to me, long-distance cyclists.

I rang the bell of the museum, housed in a bungalow where Montgomery had lived with his wife for three years. There was no answer. I rang again and, just as I did, the door was opened by the most handsome, elegant army officer I have ever had the fortune of meeting. I smiled, said hello and he brusquely asked me to wait outside. He then turned to two English people inside the museum and said:

'Thank you so much for visiting, High Commissioner. I hope you and your wife come to Quetta again soon.'

Then the commissioner, in perfectly clean, pale, pressed trousers and perfectly clean, pale, pressed skin got into a Range Rover with a tiny Union Jack on the bonnet. His wife, in a floral frock and looking like she had just finished judging victoria sponges at a school fete, gave me a withering look and followed her husband into little Britain. Oh dear, I felt like I was somehow letting the side down. They drove off, leaving me even more dusty, and the officer sighed under his breath. Or maybe I was just imagining that. I asked if I could look around the museum as I had cycled all the way from Shropshire to do just this and he, officer to the core and the corps, welcomed me inside.

You would think that a career Pakistani Army major and an English viola player would not get on very well, that the conversation would indeed be brief and awkward, but the next three hours passed in a jiffy. Uncomfortable at first, the major soon realised that I was open and honest, possibly in contrast to the people he had just been speaking with. Our conversation ranged over so many things. Looking at my diary and what I wrote about that day, one thing I noted was what excellent conversationalists so many Pakistani people are; indeed the art of conversation seemed extremely important. We talked about the English character, religion (Amir admitted to sometimes feeling more like an agnostic than a Muslim); we passed briefly over Diana's death — Amir thought Charles was responsible;

we talked about corsets, but I didn't note *what* we said about them; modern Western culture and women's rights; English people's lack of knowledge of our own history; army training (Amir thought it was essentially brainwashing); and travel. After three hours, Amir had to attend to another visitor. I had one more request of him: could I sit in Montgomery's chair? Being the perfect officer, he pulled it back from the desk for me. I sat and looked out at the view Montgomery would have taken in in the 1930s, ruminating over British India, wondering about the rise of the Nazis, feeling the aftershocks of the massive 1935 earthquake. I sat in that chair a little for me and a lot for Gran'ma.

Despite the bombings and riots and suicidal attacks, Quetta remains in my traveller's memory a Garden of Eden. The Pakistanis I met there were without exception humble, respectful and friendly.

Two wool sellers, standing proudly in their shop, coloured wool behind them, let me take their photograph, direct strong gazes for posterity.

'Bin Laden is not a terrorist!' they claimed, adding disgust and laughter at the visit of then President Clinton. This was a pre-9/11 world.

I watched the Police Bagpipe Band and wondered why young people didn't seem to learn the bagpipes; all the players were old. Maybe it was a band to retire to, or maybe it took that long to get good enough.

I had endless conversations with men who spoke in quaint English.

'What is your good name? What is your father's name? First class! What is your caste?'

Quaint English, peppered with the repeated phrases 'Thanks to God', 'If God wills it' and 'In God's name'. How calming, to speak in such a poetic, rhythmic way.

An Afghan watchmaker who had escaped his country eight years before welcomed me into his shop for tea and fixed my watch for free. I gave him my copy of *A Shropshire Lad* in return. I wondered how 'copse' and 'coppice', such essentially English things, would translate in his mind.

One morning I went and found the main post office to collect my poste restante. I was directed to the special counter — everything looking and smelling like the visa office in the High Commission in London — rang the bell and waited. After the right amount of time for somebody to finish their tea, a man's head popped up; I received my mail and a surprise invitation to visit him and his family, not back at their house, but behind the counter. There, sitting in a cupboard and looking quite content, was a small boy with a small cricket bat. I was given a stool and tea and observed the husband and wife deal with the cricket demands of an energetic toddler, the occasional foreigner requesting their mail as mere decoration to their work day. Who needs daycare, when you have a cupboard?

So the time came for me to have to leave Quetta. The hotel manager had made it very clear, so I stocked up on dried fruit and biscuits and readied myself for the journey down to the Indus Plain.

All these months I had been on a plateau, stretching from central Turkey to just west of the Indus. Quetta was still high, at about seventeen hundred metres, and tomorrow I would have to cycle one hundred and seventy kilometres through the Bolan Pass to Sibi, at one hundred and thirty metres. I would be cycling on one of the world's most dangerous roads and I would be cycling into one of the world's hottest places. Temperatures at this time of the year, in April, pre-monsoon, easily reached into the high forties and even fifties. Danger of all sorts lay ahead.

The next morning I got up before sunrise and packed up my tent. I had checked Vita the night before: pumped up her tyres, oiled her chain, checked the brake blocks and given her (that is, me) a pep talk. I had talked about how it was important to enjoy this day, to not be scared and miss the experience of cycling an historic route. From my diary, it seems I was concerned that I had somehow been a wimp thus far. Looking back now, I have no idea why I would have thought that. I look back on myself and wonder how I was ever so bold. My mother would call it rash.

All packed up, I swung my leg over Vita for this first cycling day in Pakistan. I found the road out of town, made sure I wasn't heading to the Afghan border by mistake and settled into a perfect cadence. All those days' rest had done me the world of good. My legs felt ridiculously strong and the motion of each pedal stroke was easy and light. I was a little forlorn to leave Quetta, but as the hotel manager had said, I should get out and see what else Pakistan had to offer. The final words of Amir, the army major, rang in my ears, though.

'What ever you do, don't trust the police. The army is fine, but the police are bad and corrupt.'

The shaggy city limits of Quetta drifted behind me and, after a long climb out of the valley, I started to go downhill.

C sharp major/minor/
D flat major/minor

This is it. It's the end of the road for the sharp keys. Every single note is sharp — F C G D A E B. And now, as we continue our way around the circle of fifths, the notes will be flattened in reverse. The flats are in the same order as the sharps, just back to front. We have travelled all the way from simple open G major, through the brightness of E major to the unearthliness of B major, and we have arrived in a key that stretches and strains on every instrument, even somehow the even-tempered piano. Music written in C sharp major has a wildness to it, a frenzy even. C sharp major is used by a composer who has seen a new super reality from an escarpment. They are looking through a high window, way out over our heads. It's a shocking key at first, but ultimately I find it very spiritual. It is an extremely brave and rare key; D flat major, its enharmonic sibling, is much more common for a composer to use than C sharp.

Going downhill on a bicycle has to be one of the great joys of living. It makes me think of H.G. Wells' comment that seeing an adult on a bicycle made him no longer despair for the future of the human race. It is so intrinsically fun, yet you also have to *allow* yourself to have fun. Going downhill is a serious business; a matter of balancing the thrill of going in excess of seventy kilometres an hour with very few protective clothes on, with being aware of obstacles on the road; looking up and around enough to fully experience where you are and being vigilant enough that rocks don't unseat you. And you have to be careful of your wheel rims. One day I was descending thirty kilometres from Murree, in the Karakoram foothills; it was a blistering day and I was going downhill for hours. I had to keep stopping so my rims had a chance to cool down from the constant braking, otherwise they would have warped.

When I was twenty-three, just before a Hallé Orchestra audition, I was cycling downhill to work, hit a rock, fell off and broke my arm. I missed the audition and that's why I'm not playing in an orchestra in England right now. Assuming I had won the audition.

Going downhill in animal sanctuaries in India can also have memorable moments. Cycling in the Coorg region a few years ago with my partner Jane, we were going downhill for about twenty kilometres early in the morning. I was ahead, as I'm a crazy bugger on a bike and she isn't. As I rounded one of the hairpin bends, I heard a crash and saw the flash of an animal leaping down from a tree. Jane came round the corner and we carried on, but I opted not to tell her about the sign that I had seen:

DO NOT LEAVE YOUR VEHICLE!
WILD DANGEROUS ANIMALS IN THE AREA

We didn't leave our vehicles, but it did make the next few hairpins rather interesting. Luckily the tigers and boy gangs on Enfields didn't get us, but a bumblebee did commit suicide on Jane's mouth. There's nothing like performing minor surgery on lips with the prospect of a tiger attack to focus the mind.

Down, down, down. From the top of the scale all the way to the bottom. Down through more octaves than an entire orchestra. From the high plateau to the basin of the Indus. From the piccolo to the double bass. I had always found playing descending scales harder than ascending, kind of like walking backwards, until I began to start at the top on my viola escarpment, go down to the bottom and go up again. If you make the top your home, you're happier to go there.

I was starting at the top on this day leaving Quetta and therefore the first hundred kilometres were easy. I saw the Dr Doolittle train going through the Bolan Pass tunnels, travelling slower than I was. Then, around the corner, a truck was stuck under a bridge; cars were driving up the riverbed to get round it. The road, narrow and potholed, but at least tarmacked, ran by the railway line and eventually met up properly with the Bolan

River, by now wide and shallow. An ancient boy was herding a camel train up the riverbed and wild sheep and goats ferreted among the occasional oases of reed beds. I was cycling downhill into a world that had changed very little, road and train aside, for thousands of years. And it got hotter and hotter. I was a cycling frog, slowly being boiled. I drank my bottles of water, my six-litre bag of water and was still thirsty. I filled up the bag from the river, stuck in purifying tablets, waited and drank more. If I was moving the heat was tolerable, but every time I stopped it was as if a tap had been turned on in my middle, and sweat spouted out. At the one teashop I came across I lay melting on a charpoy and drank the tea as a nectar, desperate for the sugar. And there were still so many kilometres to go before I arrived in a town. The temperature hovered around fifty. One man, greeting me from his car, asked where I was from.

'England!' I managed to say, through cracked lips.

'And how hot is it there?'

'Not more than thirty degrees …'

'Then you are very brave. This is your courage.'

With that encouragement to my courage, he sped off. Downhill too. Everything was going downhill, apart from the camels. They knew better. Who would descend onto the plain in the pre-monsoon?

The afternoon came and I cycled through a brown adobe village. The houses barely came up from the earth before they surrendered down again. I could see a group of men ahead and I prepared to be friendly, chat, maybe play them some Bach. A little lunchtime concert. As I got nearer I could see that one of the men was a policeman. Not only that, I began to realise that a rifle was slung over his shoulder and that the barrel was pointed straight at me. He stood legs wide in the middle of the road and held out his hand to make me stop. The thought did cross my mind that perhaps I could get away with not stopping. Then I remembered the man in southern Iran and trying to outrun him, and I decided to be polite. I immediately wished I wasn't so bloody polite as I smelled the breath of the policeman. He was drunk.

One of the strangest and really saddest times I have ever smelled alcohol on somebody's breath was when I was teaching music in the Vietnamese Detention Centre in Hong Kong. The music program was on Saturday mornings and Vietnamese refugees were welcome to come and take lessons. My mate Helen Therese and I taught violin, flute, theory and, bizarrely, trumpet. I had a lesson from the trumpeter in the Hong Kong Phil who gave me some pointers to look and listen out for, but to be honest, as a trumpet teacher I was a failure. Not that that was really a terrible thing; one of the main benefits of the program was to allow refugees to get away for an afternoon from the little curtained-off shelves where they lived with their families in long, sweltering tin sheds; in the music program they at least got to go to the school, which must have seemed like going abroad for a day. We had many successes at the program, young people who really improved and blossomed as musicians and who eventually were given refugee status. But there was one man who became a real problem. He, Phoang, was a trumpeter. He never practised, but hey, I wasn't exactly going to give him a hard time for that.

But he did go very red in the face on Saturdays, the sort of red that some people go when they have alcohol. It is due to a gene variant, and is a clear indicator of boozing. Either that, or he was experimenting with rouge. The only way Phoang was going to hide his drinking was if he put on a mask. I reminded him that drinking was against the music program's rules; he shrugged his shoulders and said he would see me next week. As I stood in front of him as he played the following Saturday, a waft of alcohol blew over me, with a chaser of the Haydn Trumpet Concerto. Phoang, red in the face and protesting till he was blue in the face, had to leave the program and return to the rat-infested hut. I felt awful. Phoang was eventually sent back to Vietnam, but the other people in the program, especially the young girls, breathed an alcohol-free sigh of relief.

And here was that desperate, unhappy smell again. I stood astride Vita, in front of the policeman. The small group of men looked on sullenly. Sullen wasn't good. This was a seriously faraway place and I couldn't even call the police. The trouble *was* the police. The man swayed and the group watched. I tried smiling. No. I tried chatting. No. All the time the rifle pointed at me nonchalantly, following my face and increasingly pantomime friendliness. These men, drunk as they were, must have thought they were dreaming me. I started to move off slowly, politely saying goodbye and how lovely it had been to meet them all, wishing them a good day, extracting myself from their stares and their aim. As I took a wide berth, the last of them reached out to grab my handlebars. With a deft twist I freed myself, and cycled as fast as I could with heat-affected legs. As I glanced back, the group looked bereft. Who would they tell? *What* would they tell? Who would believe them?

The episode had exhausted me and, since I was pretty much spent anyway, the rest of the journey became an enormous mental challenge. I would like to stress that this day was the only one when I had any trouble in Pakistan. I admit, though, that it was a bad day. An uphill downhill day.

Things got worse. As I approached Sibi, about ten kilometres out, men were leaving a market on their bicycles. A trio of teenagers with bolts of material on their bicycle racks and young, well-hydrated thighs propelling them, chased me and tried to grab my violin. The perfect cadence I had had in the morning with my well-rested legs was long gone. All that energy had slowly leached out over the last hundred and sixty kilometres and I could barely turn the cranks around. A man in a tractor saved me and let me hang onto the back of the trailer for the last drag into town. I had made it. I had arrived in Sibi, the only town on the whole trip where foreigners were obliged to report their arrival to the police, so dangerous was the region.

There were two hotels, opposite each other. One charged one dollar and the other two dollars. I splashed out.

In every town I had arrived in so far, and every town after this one, I felt that within the first few minutes I had made a friend. Maybe it was the hotel receptionist, somebody I had asked directions of, maybe a teashop owner, but there was always somebody who I felt I could go back to if I were in trouble. Sibi was the exception to prove this beautiful rule. The surly hotel man snatched my money, handed me a warm coke which cost as much as my room and turned back to his phone call. I heaved Vita up the stairs, barely any energy left. I knew that I had to get water and visit the police station. The room was hideous: small, airless, windowless, with brown spots on the sheets. I daren't lie down, both for the spots and the worry I would never rouse myself. I turned on the tap. Brownness leaked out. So I sat, enjoyed a moment of stillness, unpacked Vita and cycled to bottled water and the police station.

The town was still quiet after the heat of the afternoon. Dusk was falling and I cycled past silent, staring men. In the twelve or so hours I spent in Sibi, I didn't see one woman. I found the police station and cycled into the courtyard. Three policemen were standing talking and gestured me inside. They promised they would look after Vita, but for some reason I didn't believe them.

I was met by an officer, an inspector, who guided me into his office. In contrast to Amir the army major, this man was not cut from the same cloth. Even though I was utterly knackered, I still had an instinctive feel that he was not a good man. And the office was like a set from a clichéd 'imprisoned abroad' movie. The shelves were struggling valiantly with the weight of the piles of files on them, all bedraggled and limp, desperate to escape the limits of their manila folders and find a filing cabinet somewhere. There was a fan moving imperceptibly on the ceiling and all the time, throughout the whole sorry interview, two men stood at the end of the room with their arms wrenched behind them in handcuffs.

The inspector gestured for me to sit and asked for my passport. He was not actually rude, but he wasn't at all polite. By now I had fallen in love with Pakistani politeness and, by the way, I am still in love with it. This guy, though, was bored. He took my passport and, just like the Customs man at the Iran–Pakistan border, started to look very, very slowly through it. He asked me to explain why I had so many Hong Kong stamps in it; he lingered for minutes on the USA visa. He fingered the visa for India.

As he was perusing it as though it were a coffee-table book at the dentist's, I was filling in a form of foreigner registration.

All the questions were sensible enough, but there was one that grated:

Name of father

The irrelevance of this question made me so mad. My father, for whatever reason, had chosen to leave his four children when we were between the ages of two and six and a half and not visit us except for six hours a year. As we got older, that lessened to maybe six hours every three or four years. He had chosen to only once increase the measly monthly allowance he gave my mum, once in sixteen years. He had chosen to ignore the desperate problems in our family, problems that led me to want to kill myself when I was a teenager. He had chosen to not bother to send us cards or call us on our birthdays. He had chosen to not teach us to ride bicycles or to swim. He had chosen to not watch us play concerts and rugby matches. He had chosen to not have us eat dinner with him. He had chosen to not hug us every day and watch how we grew. He had chosen to not be our father; he had chosen a new family and I resented having to admit that he had taken any part in my development apart from the initial stage. My mother was my parent, and she was all I needed.

I wrote down the name of my 'father' — John Ernest George Ayres.

The inspector meanwhile had finally reached the information page at the back of my passport. He suddenly exclaimed:

'Oh, you are a woman!'

Oh no. Not now.

'Yes, I am a woman, I am wearing a men's shalwar kameez as it is more comfortable, but yes, I am indeed a woman.' I flashed what I hoped was a womanly smile.

And for the next fifteen minutes the conversation went around an increasingly frightening circle of me saying I was a woman, and the inspector saying that I was a very attractive woman, but then changing his mind and saying he could hardly believe I was a woman. It was all getting very, very worrying. He didn't seem to want to relent and I had lost the one thing I could rely on in these situations — a sense of humour. What could I do? I thought about getting a female officer and showing her my breasts. It was unlikely there was one. Officer I mean, not breast. I thought maybe I could call the High Commission and speak to somebody working with the man with the pale, pressed skin. All these things seeped through my dehydrated and starved brain. I had arrived in fifty degrees and a severely unfriendly town, and I wanted my mum.

The intensity of the inspector's disbelief seemed to go up a notch; as it did, a policeman from the courtyard came in and said something in Urdu. The inspector leapt up, leaving my passport on his overflowing desk. I grabbed my chance. I had filled in the form; I had done everything asked of me except prove my gender. I seized my passport and left the office and the two bowed prisoners. In the courtyard the policemen were riding Vita around in the dust and the dusk. I put on my best impression of an English school ma'am, brusquely asked them to dismount, swung my leg over and left the police station. As I left they shouted after me. They knew where I was staying, they even knew the room number. This was going to be a long night.

I made it back to the hotel and threw up. I just about managed to take off my cycling shorts, rinse them and drag out my silk sleeping sack. I climbed into it, lay on top of the brown spots and watched the evening fall through the skylight. I had never felt so alone and so vulnerable in my life. Sleep didn't come the whole night. I read a little, but mostly lay there feeling scared and thinking of a strategy if the police came knocking. Really, I had none. Feeling scared is so debilitating. The panic, the racing heart, but also the feeling of mental and physical weakness and lack of ability to control your destiny. When I went to Kabul in 2013 I was scared of possible bombings and attacks, but then got so frustrated with myself that I managed to talk myself out of it. In Sibi I didn't. In the hour dawn came, I finally slept. I never, ever want to go back to that place.

C sharp major turns to D flat major. Seven sharps to five flats. Bright light on top of the escarpment changes to dappled light deep in the forest. D flat major is the key of solace, of endings, of acceptance in the inevitable. Beethoven used D flat in the slow movement of his final quartet, Opus 135.

Beethoven wrote his final quartet in the last six months of his life; it was his last major work. Not only was Beethoven struggling with shocking health and profound deafness, but his nephew Karl had also tried to commit suicide. When you hear the final quartet, however, it is like listening to an old man who has found young love; he returns to the classical forms of his youth and, in the final movement, now in F major (also the key of his first published quartet), he asks the question:

'*Muss es sein?*'

'Must it be?'

Must what be? Nobody knows. It is a musical koan that Beethoven monks have studied and meditated on for aeons. Must Beethoven pay his housekeeper every Saturday morning, as he complained about and apparently sang about? Must death be? Must a perfect cadence be? The question is asked with an augmented fourth, the devil's interval, and is asked repeatedly throughout the final movement. Then, in the last few bars, Beethoven skips off stage and answers the question with a mischievous, swift, perfect cadence, as if life were only ever sound and fury, signifying nothing.

From F major in the first movement, the key drops a major third, to D flat.

The viola starts. An F, no longer the tonic, now the major third of the chord. Then, after a long dotted crotchet, the second violin with an A flat, the fifth. Then the first violin with the tonic, the D flat. And finally the cello, first finger all the way down down down on the bottom string with the lowest possible tonic as the bedrock. The first violin adds another major third, so that we are quite sure of where we are and the four parts sit there for an endless while.

And then, a magical moment; possibly the most magical moment in the whole of the quartet repertoire: the first violin plays, on the G string, a simple melody that is essentially the D flat major scale. But it is so much more. Beethoven originally gave this movement the title 'Sweet Song of Rest or Peacefulness'. You feel as if you are dropping to the bottom of the ocean, but it's all right; you have relinquished your desire for light and for living. Beethoven is with you and his music guides you gently down, a hand underneath your head as the softest pillow. And you surrender. This is surely music to die to.

After that night in Sibi I felt cleansed and light. Something huge had shifted in my head and I headed out into the bright daylight; the catharsis of that emotional and physical intensity had left me hollowed out. I now see that day of downhill as a turning point in my life; I had survived. I had done it on my own and I finally respected myself. No longer would I accuse myself of being a wimp.

It took a while to recover physically from the downhill day. I had to hole up in a hotel in Larkana for five days with what was probably sunstroke. An horrific headache, extreme nausea, stomach ache and utter exhaustion. The first night of sickness, all I could do to ignore the pain in my head and stomach was walk from one end of the room to the other, a wraith-like tread. I slept, and watched the BBC World Service, the endless news cycle giving a range of cadences through those sick days.

When I finally emerged from my room, another guest, a stout young man who was staying in the hotel to study for his civil service exams, greeted me. He was very concerned for my health; his home was nearby and he called his wife, asked her to make some khichri and have it sent over by their servant.

The English adopted khichri and turned it into kedgeree, the smoked fish and rice dish. The original khichri is a simple dish for invalids and old people, and it is generally the first solid food babies eat. Rice is cooked with lentils and is very delicately flavoured, ideally with just a little ginger and turmeric. The rice and daal are over-cooked till mushy, and then served with yoghurt. All quite different from the stiff kedgeree of my childhood.

Farooq knocked on my door and announced that the khichri had arrived. I went round to his room, still feeling a little light on my legs and sat down in front of a wide thermos. Farooq unscrewed its lid with his massive, delicately manicured hand; inside the thermos was a mound of the lightest rice and daal, almost diaphanous. Just smelling it was healing. I dipped a spoon into it and dropped some onto my tongue. I think one of my taste buds is still in heaven. It is a dish I turn to again and again when I am ill, remembering the taste of Farooq's wife's khichri. Never quite reproducing it, but coming close enough to being able to imagine it. Like a concert performance that is never equalled on a CD.

Farooq was charming, urbane and sophisticated. We talked about literature — the classics, and books like *Small Is Beautiful*, by E.F. Schumacher. This was voted one of the most influential books of the post-war period and deals not only with economics but the health of society, something that economists so often seem to forget. The endless 'bigger is better' is totally trounced in the book, with an emphasis on intermediate technology being the sustainable way forward. Technology that the average person can fix at home. When you think of our reliance on computers and smartphones, you wonder what Schumacher would have made of our progress. Farooq was hoping to win a place in the prestigious Pakistani Civil Service and help with the transition of Pakistan away from a feudal society. He was a modern man who believed in the stability of marriage; he had married his cousin.

Farooq and I walked through the topic of Western values being irrelevant in an Eastern country. Is democracy the best system for Pakistan? Is it the best system for *every* country? Is it not rather arrogant of the West to think that it is? And is there such a thing as a country's karma, or fate, to be always governed by the same sort of system, but in a different guise — Russia and the Tsars, then Stalin for instance? If so, what was Pakistan's fate?

A political writer once wrote that Pakistan was not a country, but a crowd; my experience was that if it were a crowd, it was the politest and most hospitable and intelligent crowd (Sibi aside) that I had ever been a part of. Young men in Pakistan constantly impressed me; men who educated themselves and improved their lives and avoided the Islamic repression that was evident in some places. Amir, the army major, had pointed out that since the Quran is in Arabic, and since many young people didn't speak Arabic, they were at the mercy of mullahs who interpreted the Quran in questionable ways.

Women in Pakistan, though, were like absent notes in the scale, D naturals in a D flat world. I hardly met any. Even in private homes I was only invited to talk with the men; women looked at me from a distance. Literally from another room. It seemed I had more in common with their men than with them.

The day after the khichri I wrapped myself up against the heat and took a bus to Mohenjo-Daro, close to the Indus. Mohenjo-Daro is an ancient city (2500BC) built on a ridge overlooking the flood plain of the Indus; it would have originally been right beside the Indus. The name means 'Mound of the Dead', but that's not its original name; that has been lost. A Buddhist monk had thought that this mound was a stupa, and led an Indian archaeologist, Rakhaldas Bandyopadhyay, to the site in 1922; Bandyopadhyay went on to become a great scholar and writer of Indian historical fiction. Mohenjo-Daro is considered the finest example of the Indus civilisation, although archaeologists warn that if it is not properly conserved, the entire city could be lost by 2030. If you are reading this in 2031, is it still there?

The bejewelled bus dropped me off below a low hill and I walked through a thick blanket of swelter to the ticket office; it was fifty degrees. Here was a place that was as old as the oldest pyramids and you could still walk its streets and feel its fired bricks. There were (understandably) very few people there. I felt like the final survivor, walking through the grid-pattern streets, looking down into the great bath and up into the granary. Mohenjo-Daro was probably an administrative centre, with strong similarities to the other city of this time, Harappa. Harappa was slowly whittled away, literally brick by brick, to make other cities, but Mohenjo-Daro was closer to good easy rock pickings, so it survived. The change in the course of the Indus was its undoing, as trade moved elsewhere and the city became eventually not even a backwater, but a beyond-the-backwater. The contrast in the quiet, ordered, clean and austere past with the chaotic present couldn't have been more, well, wonderful, though Mohenjo-Daro was falling down because of lack of government care, with little to prop it up; a Pompeii of Pakistan. It would soon be a memory.

Sometimes I think about all the music we listen to and perhaps take for granted and wonder what would happen if, for instance, suddenly by some freak event every single score and part and recording of Beethoven's Fifth Symphony disappeared. If Beethoven's bricks were all stolen, would there be enough people in the world to recreate the second trombone part, or the viola part? What happens when a whole culture is on the verge of disappearing and all we have are memories?

That was the case in Kabul in 2001, by the time the Mujahideen and the Taliban had finished with the musicians of Afghanistan. Afghan music had been kept alive by a few musicians overseas and a very few brave souls in Afghanistan itself, but the music, like Mohenjo-Daro, was in danger of crumbling back down into the earth.

One of the musicians who Dr Sarmast invited to teach at the Afghanistan National Institute of Music (ANIM) was Ustad Irfan Khan. 'Ustad' is an Urdu term for a master and Irfan is from Lucknow in India, his family having come from Afghanistan many generations before. One of his ancestors had been a horse trader who had travelled to India for business and met the legendary musician Tansen's great grandson. Tansen was said to be so great a singer that if he sang a raga for the monsoon it would instantly rain, and a raga for the winter, a chill would lace the summer air. Tansen's great grandson played to the Ustad's great grandfather, and he was entranced. He wanted to play Indian classical music on his Afghan instrument, the rubab, but he was laughed out of the court (I know how that feels) as the rubab only has a limited range. The rubab is plucked, with three melody strings and many sympathetic strings. The body is made from a single piece of mulberry wood and it is known as the 'Lion of Instruments'. Its drawback, for Indian music, is its small range and lack of subtle pitch changes.

And so the story is told of how Niyamatullah Khan invented the sarod to have a suitable, more versatile instrument for Indian classical music; derived from the rubab, it has a similar-shaped body, but with a metal fingerboard and no frets. It has a much bigger range than the rubab, and strings that vibrate in sympathy. The sound is exquisite, smooth and clean, with a hint of metal but a lot of earth, as the top of the body is made of goatskin.

Ustad Khan had taught in Kabul in the 1980s, but his

students had either moved overseas or been killed in the war. If he didn't come back to teach and revive the sarod, it would be balanced on the verge of extinction. And how would you extract DNA to clone sarod music, one hundred years hence? So, fortunately for Afghan music, Ustad Khan had returned to Kabul and had been teaching at the institute for three years. The Ustad was succeeding in his singularly important mission. Both girls and boys were learning the instrument and the sound of music on the sarod, with a particular Afghan touch, is heard again in the music school in the west of Kabul.

C sharp minor shares the key signature of E major, with an added B sharp for the leading note, or seventh degree of the scale. Every note or degree of the Western scale has a name: tonic, supertonic, mediant, subdominant, dominant, submediant, leading note then back to tonic.

Do is tonic, re is supertonic etc. Tonic a deer, a female deer, supertonic a drop of golden sun … it just doesn't work, does it? Hence 'do re mi'; I particularly love the word supertonic though. There should be a band called The Supertonics. And in a garage far, far away, there probably is.

The leading note is a semitone or half step below the tonic. If you just use a shared key signature for the minor scale, you get a natural minor, which leaves you with a whole step between the tonic and the leading note. There's nothing wrong with that, but if you want a lot of tension, and to really feel the stretch between the two notes, paradoxically it's better to raise that leading note. That's why minor keys will have extra sharps or naturals in the music (accidentals) to make the leading note higher. Hence B sharp.

The *Moonlight Sonata* is probably the most famous piece of music in C sharp minor. It's probably the most famous piece of piano music, full stop. The opening triplets of the famous first movement are initially calming; they lull you, despite being in a minor key, until you realise there is actually dark intent lurking underneath them. That intent becomes clear with the melody in the right hand; such a simple figure, more about the rhythm than the pitch; it's a figurative hand that initially caresses, then presses too hard, an insistence that turns from sweet lullaby to cruel force. The first two notes, with their dotted rhythm, clash immediately with the smoothness of the triplets. Six G sharps are played before the melody changes to an A, then a deft move to E major. As if nothing ever happened. Such intensity in so few notes is not too far removed from Webern and his imploded star-like *Six Bagatelles*.

Embassies in Kabul regularly invite the musicians from ANIM to come and play for them. Names of performers and car registration numbers are faxed to and fro and the Afghan students dress in their very finest clothes and perform for countries' diplomats, who will occasionally donate money. The Americans donate a huge amount, the Australian Government very little, despite Dr Sarmast being an Australian and the musicians playing at the Australia Day Party in 2013. Hours are spent sitting in choked-up traffic to go across town to the embassies' secure zone and then be searched and quizzed by dismissive security guards. The musicians, all of whom are Muslim, have to suffer their instruments being sniffed and touched by dogs, an unclean animal for them.

As I write this, the troop withdrawal has been announced and a 'bitter-sweet victory' declared. Many, many billions of dollars have been spent on fighting Afghans, and so many lives have been lost. What would happen if, as Anne Deveson beseeches, we had waged peace in the last twelve years, rather than war? If we had truly waged peace, rather than it being a counterpoint to the main theme of killing?

One evening I went along to the German Embassy with some of the musicians. The registration number of our bus was incompatible with the embassy's list, so we had to stand outside the embassy in minus ten degrees until they allowed us to walk in through the steel cages and bombproof enclosures. Once inside and greeted by overly courteous diplomats, Elham, a brilliant young pianist, played a tarantella, and some of the teachers performed a Schubert piece. Listening to Schubert and sitting beside beer-sipping soldiers with remarkably clean combat boots seemed incongruous, especially when you considered the hardships people were enduring outside the concrete, barbed-wired walls. The combat boots had been wiped clean of any war and Schubert seemed to highlight the fragility of society. We were in a fortress and the walls that evening seemed not only to be made of concrete, but also of music. Music can be a mode of lifting us from our earthly roots, but it can also be a way of ignoring the truth. That night it felt like both. As we left, and the rude guards handed back cameras and phones, Milat, a very fine pianist with hair the colour of the midnight sky, pointed up at the clear dark night and the new moon.

'I'm going to play that sonata one day.'

I left Larkana, cured by khichri, tea, air-conditioning and kindness.

Every day on this journey I woke up with excitement, thrilled by the thought of the adventures I would be having that day, assured that I would always be moving forward and that no day would ever be boring. After the downhill day that awakening feeling had taken a battering, but on this morning it was back, emerging from the wreck of the last few days like the horn solo in the final movement of Beethoven's Sixth Symphony.

Some of the farmers I played Bach to in Pakistan. They would sit very still and break out in huge smiles at the end, then want to have a go themselves.

I started cycling at six, just as the sun was coming over the wheat fields. The first adventure was being invited into a police station for an extra-sweet cup of tea. I cycled past camels with patterns shaved into their coats and donkeys with sores crushed into theirs. Wheat fields, date palms, irrigation canals beside the road. As the heat fell and the morning acquiesced, I napped beside the canal, miles from any village. When I woke, two farmers, sitting with their hand scythes, were waiting patiently to ask me what was my good name, and what was in my violin case. My route through Pakistan is an invisible yet still faintly audible line marked by small, canal-side lunchtime concerts, to audiences of two or three farmers at a time.

I passed through the village birthplace of Zulfikar Ali Bhutto, prime minister and father of Benazir. By this time I had realised that Pakistanis love Bach and his vigorousness; in fact, I had come to expect a request for a little piece every time I stopped, which is why, when I turned off the main road to check out Bhutto's birthplace and have a little cup of tea, I thought I might have a play too.

It was teatime. Oh, okay, it's always teatime in Pakistan. That's one of the things I love about it. I skidded Vita to a stop and asked for tea at the tiny stall. As soon as I did, and I wonder whether tests have been conducted as to how this can be humanly possible, what seemed like the entire male population of the village was right next to me, a bubble of questions. Little kids stood on my toes and peered at my violin case and there it came, the classic tap on the case, the shrug of the arms and the request for me to play something. I took out Aurelia, who was quite used to the heat by now, and played the Bach Bourrée. Except I couldn't, because the kids were crowding around me so tightly that I couldn't bow without poking them in the head. Teashop by teashop, I was becoming part of the crowd of Pakistan.

I reached Sukkur in the full heat of the day; I found a hotel and as I was heaving Vita up the steps a foreign woman asked:

'Oh, are you cycling in Pakistan?'

'No. No I'm not. What would make you think such a thing? What this is, is a test I'm conducting in various countries to see what inane questions people ask. But I also like carrying fully loaded touring bikes up steep steps in fifty-degree heat after cycling one hundred kilometres.'

Okay, that wasn't out loud. Only a groan of incredulity.

I was excited to arrive in Sukkur because it was home to two curious things on the river: a huge barrage across the Indus, the world's largest in fact, which I would get to cycle across, and a Hindu temple which had survived Partition. I unpacked my bags and headed over to the district commissioner's office to ask for permission to visit the temple. A Hindu clerk greeted me (I knew he was Hindu because he had 'ohm' tattooed on his hand, but thanks for asking) and he regrettably informed me that I was too late to visit the temple as it was a Friday and it was closed after midday. But would I like to pay a courtesy call on the district commissioner?

Why yes I would. So I did, though I should perhaps add at this point that I was extremely scruffy on this day. I mean, even under these new standards of international cycling, I was scruffy. You can probably imagine the sort of level of grub we are talking about. I hadn't really had a chance to wash before

I went out again and frankly I wouldn't have wanted to invite myself anywhere; so when this kind young man was very polite and suggested I make a courtesy call to the highest official in the district I was, to say the least, a little uncomfortable.

I was shown into a large air-conditioned office. At the far end sat five men, four in front in various uniforms, and one in civilian clothes behind an enormous desk, which was covered with a large-scale map of the town. The clerk introduced me to the assembly, and the district commissioner (the one behind the desk), trouser creases and hair parting perfect, gestured for me to come and sit next to him. His name was Qaleem and he continued the meeting, politely looking at me from time to time to check I wasn't bored. How could I be? I had a ringside seat at a security meeting for a local festival. Sunni Muslims are in the majority in Pakistan and the Festival was a Shia one. In the past (I had been filled in by Qaleem) there had been scuffles and even a riot, so it was serious business making sure security was tight. Present was the head of the police, the head of the army, an army major and Qaleem's deputy. The lieutenant colonel was deadpan, the major keen and little. They spoke a fascinating mixture of language; they rattled away in Urdu and Sindhi then suddenly the English words 'security barrier' broke out, along with 'encroachment' and 'risk', all with fabulously rolled rrrrr's. As I sat listening to these men discuss such crucial details, I thought of the English General Sir Charles James Napier who led British forces when they captured the whole Sindh Province (including Sukkur) in the 1840s. He is said to have sent a single-word telegram to the king — 'Peccavi'. Latin for 'We have sinned/Sindh'. It turns out the general wasn't such a wit after all — it was a subscriber to *Punch* magazine who had written the pun.

The meeting was finally over, although I could have sat there all day observing the interplay, dominance and compromise of the soldiers, the police and the civilian officials. A living, breathing version of rock-paper-scissors.

Qaleem invited me to stay for lunch and offered me a glass of water. He sat and watched me as I drank it and declared the world would, in years to come, fight over water. This was the first time I had heard such a theory and of course he will be, has been, proved correct. The slaking property of the water seemed heightened by Qaleem's gaze. A servant then came into the office bearing a dish of chicken biryani. A single, simple dish of meat and rice; the way it was cooked, how the spices were balanced and the rice grains individually separated by the oil, I have never had, and possibly could not bear to have, such a delectable biryani since. Experiences while travelling are so special that sometimes we want to recreate them, but then you try and that somehow takes away from the initial experience and lessens it. It takes discipline to say to yourself, 'That is enough. I have had that experience; it will not be equalled or bettered.'

Qaleem enquired where I was staying. I said that I had checked into a pretty good hotel in town and was very happy there, but he insisted I stay at a government guesthouse as his guest. I politely declined, not wanting to put him to any trouble, but he insisted and said he would send his man over to move my things. So I accepted and was invited to spend the afternoon at the guesthouse waiting out the heat of the day, then go for a drive around town with Qaleem in the evening. So, after having arrived at the offices in the morning on Vita who was pretty grubby herself, I was driven away in a spanking clean Land Cruiser with a fluttering Pakistani flag on the bonnet, Vita in the back and an armed guard with rifle between his knees sitting next to the driver. As I left the car I looked back at my seat to make sure I had not left any grub behind, or colour, like George Trikilis on the aeroplane.

I napped through the afternoon at the guesthouse, which had been built by the British in the 1920s for the chief engineer of the barrage, Sir Charlton Harrison. The barrage is still very much in use, irrigating the Thar Desert and controlling the largest irrigation system in the world, with some of the seven canals leading from it larger than the Suez Canal. At the time it was being built it was the largest civil engineering project in the world. That meant the chief engineer had to have a pretty flash place to stay and the bungalow really was, made from brick with enormous, high-ceilinged rooms and huge, panoramic windows. Qaleem came at about six, as the heat was beginning to pretend it had never really been there. The evenings in Pakistan, pre-monsoon, were similar to what I now experience of Australian evenings in the summer: long and with a feeling of a new day after the exhaustion of the white heat. We sat and drank tea under an enormous willow tree, looking out to the Indus just metres away. I played Qaleem my violin and he exclaimed in enthusiasm at the music and the instrument. I had spent so long playing beautiful music with fine players in specially built concert halls, yet there, in a garden in Pakistan, for the first time for a long time, I heard music for its singular magic.

The mosquitoes started to bite, so we drove out of town to see some ancient tombs. The nomads who had built them left nothing else behind. This was their only mark on the world, sandstone tombs.

That evening was such a balm after the downhill day and the fever in Larkana. I was better physically, but that night made me better emotionally. Qaleem was again a highly educated man who had strong opinions about matters, but who also welcomed robust conversation and listened to a different viewpoint. He told me about how Pakistan got its name from the regions of the old Raj: P – Punjab; A – Afghan Province (North West Frontier); K – Kashmir; S – Sindh; and stan from Balochistan. The 'i' was added as a pronunciation aid. One of the things we travelled through in our eight-hour conversation was physiognomy; Qaleem was the district magistrate and in all the years he had sat on the bench, he had come to read people's faces as clearly as a musician reads a score. He believed you could tell a lot about somebody by their ears, a certain size and shape indicating, for Qaleem, different levels of criminality and honesty. I feel mine as I write this and wonder why they bend over so easily. The conversation with Qaleem was the equal of the conversation with the army major; both men keen to listen, keen to share, curious and searingly intelligent.

I had a beer that night, the first time in three months. Beer brewed in Lahore and brought to me on a tray with a chilled glass by a servant with the most severely crossed eyes I have ever seen. I marvelled that he did his job so beautifully. The best beer is on a hot day after riding a bike a very long way; beer was unavailable in these last few months so I had developed a tea habit instead of a beer habit. Considering the amount of sugar in the tea, it was hardly a healthy choice.

In the bungalow, beside the Indus, I slept with a feeling of being blessed. The more I travelled in Pakistan, the more I loved it — the extraordinary things that happened every day, like a policeman on the side of the road grabbing my thigh (he called me sir), being very impressed with my cycling efforts, then giving me a shove up the hill. And having my hair cut by a ten-year-old boy with scissors as large as his head.

The same feeling happens with a key in the end. I remember I was appalled the first time I had to play a scale of D flat major. You have to put your first finger where? Sorry, how many flats? Then, once I had settled down into the key, like settling inside a yoga pose or a friendship, I couldn't imagine ever being uncomfortable there and I also couldn't imagine ever wanting to be in any other key. Some keys do work differently on different instruments, though. For instance, the French horn works well with flat keys, B flat or E flat, as that is, or is close to, their fundamental note. They don't like sharp keys so much, although a skilled player will of course be able to play in F sharp very happily. String instruments work slightly better in sharp keys, but pianos are very happy in a key like D flat major, as it fits the hand well with the black keys. A piece like Chopin's Nocturne in D Flat falls under your fingers and sounds easy and glacé-like on the piano. Easy, like breathing out.

I felt like Pakistan was the right key for me. I didn't want to ever leave Pakistan, or at least lose the feeling Pakistan had given me. One of the things I had grown to love doing was simply sitting and thinking in the evening. That, or making up words to foreign TV series. Sitting and thinking, and letting my mind wander through the day, or the place or a piece of music, wherever it wanted to go; it was bliss. The opposite to meditation, I suppose. I tried meditation for a while and I couldn't do it, because that blissful feeling of free wondering beckoned to me too insistently. Then I was introduced to Vipassana meditation and my whole outlook changed. I can't recommend Vipassana keenly enough. If it calls to you, do it.

As we end the enharmonic keys, I end with a story of enharmonic gender.

As Pakistan fell under my fingers and my pedals and wheels, I eventually found myself in Bahawalpur. On leaving Sukkur I had stayed in government guesthouses for two nights (where they wouldn't even let me pay) and been welcomed by the military and the police, who were behaving themselves much better than the police in Sibi.

I was now in the state of five rivers — the Punjab, or Panjab. *Panj* (five), *ab* (water). The heat was made tolerable by going into a petrol station every hour or so to cool down. There was a striking contrast between the varied road rules, quality of road surface, types of vehicles and styles of driving on the Pakistani highways, and the ordered, foreign, air-conditioned petrol stations owned by Shell and Caltex. The modernisation of Pakistan was arriving in surprising ways, although the tea at Caltex was rubbish and they didn't have any charpoys.

Bahawalpur, still on the Indus, was a town of several princely palaces. I arrived there around midday and had a bit of trouble finding a hotel. A young man, who seemed to be driving his grandma around, stopped his car and asked if he could help me. I asked where there was a hotel and he very kindly invited me to follow him and he would lead me to one. I did, and we made a short procession through the town, with Grandma looking back to check I was keeping up. We arrived at a suitable-looking, cheery hotel and I thanked Aqbal and his grandma. Aqbal suggested we meet later, post-nap and afternoon heat, and he and his friend would drive me around the town. Sounded good to me. I checked in, washed myself, washed my cycling/sleeping/lounging shirt, napped and waited for Aqbal to return.

He came on the dot, at 6.30, and commented that I was wearing the same shirt and wouldn't it be better to change after cycling? I reassured him that despite looking grubby, I was as clean as I could be with limited packing space, and we took off. Aqbal's friend Haroon sat in the front, and we drove around town. Bahawalpur is a university town of just under a million people and they all seemed to be out in the evening. The restaurants and ice-cream parlours were full of students, joyful in the balm of the dropping sun. We stopped for ice-cream, drove around some of the high walls of the palaces and then Aqbal asked me:

'Emmett, do you have a girlfriend?'

185

Emmett was the name many Pakistani people called me, as it was the name they heard when I said 'Emma'. Because I was travelling on my own and was wearing men's clothes and am quite sturdy, most people assumed I was a bloke (remember Sibi), especially when they heard 'Emmett', which is in fact a Pakistani name. This didn't bother me at all, as I was meeting most of these people briefly and often it would have been simply too confusing to explain otherwise. Officials were a different story, but when Aqbal asked me this question, which revealed he thought I was a man, I was terribly conflicted. Well, I suppose he could have been wise to a lesbian's androgynous appearance, but I doubted it. I had just spent the last two hours with two polite young men driving around a foreigner whom they believed to be, as I saw clearly now, a man. I should have realised before and told them, but by now it was too late. If I corrected them they would have felt guilty for spending all that time with a foreign woman and I didn't want to upset them. So I kept as close to the truth as I could and said yes. In a very low voice.

And it was true. At the time I was going out with a beautiful American flautist who was living in New York; so that's what I said, but in the back seat I shrank with the deceit of my gender.

There is a long history of women dressed in men's clothes, living their lives as men. One of the most famous was Dr James Barry, who joined the British Army, became Surgeon General and lived for seventy years until 1865. James' physical gender was only discovered after death. Earlier than James, women have dressed as men and fought in wars, gone to sea as sailors and been husbands. Perhaps it was a lesbian way of getting around marriage laws (and how crazy that we would have to do that even today), but perhaps it was also just a way of being accepted into a man's world. A way of moving beyond men treating you differently, whether well or badly. How these men/women were treated by women — that is another question. In Pakistan, the very few women I met knew instantly that I was Emma, not Emmett. Moving through Pakistan the men I met casually treated me with enormous bonhomie and openness, something that I think would not have happened if they knew I was a woman. Qaleem, the district commissioner, was extremely polite, but there was a reserve, in contrast with another day when I sat talking to two soldiers from Quetta for hours; they called me Emmett and I felt at the end of our conversation that we had had the most amazing male bonding. Maybe it isn't exclusive to seemingly men-only company, but I have never had the same feeling with men again. I was beginning to understand the simple power of male relationships. I now look at men talking with each other and I am glad that I know a little something of their world, and consider myself lucky to be one of the few women who does. A woman who has been a man, and gone back again.

'Lucky you!' said Aqbal.

Haroon nodded and they said how hard it was for them to meet girls. If they managed to, all they could do was talk on the phone. Aqbal wondered if I would like to visit his father at their house. In for a penny, in for a pound, I thought. And that extreme politeness of not wanting to hurt their feelings meant that I, of course, said yes. In a very low voice. They called me their brother.

We drove to Aqbal's house, set in a courtyard in a middle-class part of town. Aqbal brought us inside and explained that we would not go to the women's side of the house, but just stay in the men's side. Aqbal's father stood up from his daybed and shook my hand with glee. He was very pleased to meet me and invited me to sit down next to him on the bed. I did so, and was glad of my small breasts, my hairy legs, my broadish shoulders, my low voice, my short hair and the looseness of a shalwar kameez. We proceeded to have yet another extraordinary conversation. My leg muscles were admired and squeezed and Aqbal's dad was so relaxed at one point, talking about how hard it was to get visas for the UK, that he said:

'Fuck you and fuck your nation!'

Fair enough. It seemed that the British were taking a lot of money from people for visas, but eventually not approving them for immigration. Aqbal's dad wasn't going to give up, though. He wanted to know where was the best place to invest in the UK. Um, probably best to not ask a musician. Aqbal's dad, on discussing marriage, said:

'Divorce is the most hated thing which is permitted.'

As I got up to leave, the father reminded me quite sincerely that if I was having any trouble at all in Pakistan I should without question give him a call. He called me his son and swung me into an enormous bear hug. All I could think about was whether he might notice my breasts.

A flat major/minor

As I became more comfortable on my journey, the end of it began to loom uncomfortably. What was I going to do after my trip?

When I was studying at the Royal Academy in London my quartet had gone through a huge crisis. Our first violinist had had a nervous breakdown due to terrible bullying from her father, and I had wanted to give up playing the viola; I think I was burnt out. So Mr White, my teacher, sat me down and got me to write a list of pros and cons of being a viola player. All I can remember from that list was that travel was at the top of the pro column. And so I had continued to play the viola. There was no Mr White here in the Himalayan foothills to help me now. I was going to have to work it out on my own.

As I climbed higher and higher in Pakistan, I began to cycle through career options in my mind. Go back to university, but to do what? Study Russian again, but then what to do with it? Join the army as a musician? Become a bike mechanic? Go back to playing in an orchestra? I had no idea, but the future was no longer invisible and avoidable.

The cello and my long dream of learning to play it ambled around in my head; I came across it in unexpected moments, as a melody singing inside my mind. As the pedals turned, my thoughts tumbled around the risk of giving up the viola completely and playing through another interrupted cadence by choosing the cello.

I had chosen the cello when I was eight. Now I was thirty-three, wasn't it time I did what I wanted? And wasn't it time to either let the cello go, or just go for it?

My journey so far had been emotionally hard and physically demanding because of the temperature in Pakistan, but once I had gained some fitness, the cycling had become, well, easy really. My pedal cadence was swift and unstressful, with a perfectly balanced pull up of one pedal as I pushed down on the other. The only parts of my body that protested now were the heels of my hands, as they went numb from so much leaning on them. I improvised by putting thick socks on my handlebars. And so Vita and I made our way higher, higher and higher. Through Lahore, a side-trip to India and then, eventually, back to Islamabad, up to Murree and over the foothills of the western Himalayas looking towards Kashmir, and a steep descent on a back road (forty kilometres without pedalling) to Abbottabad.

Abbottabad is now probably most famous for being the town where Osama bin Laden was killed by a team of American special forces soldiers. Who knows, maybe he was living there back in 2000 with his wives and children, daringly hidden in plain sight behind the military college. Who would have noticed him in the town, among the thousands of tourists who come flocking in the summer to escape the heat of the Indus Plain? Would he have heard their vacation joy over the walls of his compound? And how come somebody who hid inside for so long didn't suffer from vitamin D deficiency? Maybe he did.

I stayed the night in Abbottabad (I don't think with bin Laden) and on the way north out of town the next day I stopped at an Internet café to check my mail. Just as I was leaving, an extremely handsome and rich-looking young man asked me where I was heading on my bicycle. I described my route and my destination. Sometimes, when people asked me this question, I didn't say 'Hong Kong' as I had realised people didn't always believe me. There was a look on their face of 'of yeah, right'. Or else a confused look, not knowing where Hong Kong was, or indeed what it was. This reaction was mirrored when I had finished my trip and people asked me what I had been doing for the last year. I rarely said:

'Oh, I've been cycling on my own from Shrewsbury to Hong Kong. Yes, over a few deserts, five-thousand-metre passes, yes through Iran and Pakistan.'

I found it became an isolating statement. People often didn't know what to ask, where to even begin to ask about it. Indeed I, for a long time, didn't know where to begin to talk about it.

That's why it has taken thirteen years to write this book. Many people asked, 'Why did you do it?' And I would answer:

'To find out why.'

Amir, I sensed, would receive this unusual news with equanimity. He didn't blink an eye and asked me straight away if I would like to visit his mother.

Up to this point I had met very few women in Pakistan. On the street, women were too shy to talk to me (so different from Iran) and in private houses the women came and served us drinks, then left immediately. If I caught their eye they would look confused, as they were smarter than their men and *they* realised I was Emma, not Emmett. So when Amir invited me to meet his mum, I couldn't wait. Such an intelligent, handsome polite boy would surely have an extraordinary mother, especially if he were so keen for me to meet her. We did the by now familiar thing of him driving slowly and me following on Vita. I was ahead of schedule for leaving the country on time for my visa, so I hoped I would be able to spend some time with the family.

Amir drove up to an elegant white house and went inside. And with a scurry of noise and bustle, out burst a large, tall, big-boned woman in shalwar kameez who came and gave me an enormous kiss. There was no problem with Emma/Emmett here. She, Fatima, enveloped me in her arms and we spent the rest of the day delighting in each other's company. We had lunch, and then drove to meet Fatima's brother who had been a soldier in the war between East and West Pakistan in 1971.

When Pakistan was formed after Partition, it was split between the west, where Pakistan as it is now known is, and the east, which is now Bangladesh. The East Pakistanis were becoming increasingly infuriated with being treated as second-class citizens by the West and decided to declare independence. Soldiers loyal to the West fought defecting soldiers and independence fighters; eventually the Indian Army joined in against West Pakistan and soon Dhaka was lost and the West surrendered. West Pakistani soldiers surrendered at the racecourse in Dhaka — the largest number of prisoners of war since the Second World War — and were eventually sent home to the West. It was a huge loss for Pakistan and paved the way for Zulfikar Ali Bhutto to take power.

Fatima's brother was in his fifties, strong and small with perfect white teeth. He had the delightful face of a TV comedian from the sixties. He spoke so excitedly of that time in Dhaka; there was no sense of dishonour in losing. He had been in a place, at the Dhaka racecourse, where history had been made and he was proud of that. I was getting a sense of Pakistanis actually not being a crowd at all. That writer who had dismissed Pakistan as a mere crowd had been wrong. The Pakistanis I met were immensely patriotic, they were very suspicious of India (and China), they knew their country's problems and they loved the country so much that they were prepared to fight for its survival. If that meant occasionally fighting each other, so be it.

Fatima took Amir and me to the top of one of the hills surrounding Abbottabad. It really is a beautiful town. You might say that Rome is the Abbottabad of Europe. You might, for the similarity of the hills, but you probably won't. We looked out onto the garrisons, schools, colleges and parks as the light slipped away behind us. Somewhere would have been Osama bin Laden's compound. That nightmare was yet to come for these elegant people.

In the evening Fatima plugged in the video player, invited the whole extended family over for a feast and we sat for hours watching a wedding video. It was the edited highlights, coming in at just under three hours.

Fatima was a force of womanhood. She dreamt of going paragliding in the Maldives and had given one of her children to a family member, as they 'had no issue'. She wanted the very best for her son Amir, so she was sending him to the US to study I.T. at university. Her husband was quiet and obedient, very earnest about religion and repeating that mullahs often misinterpreted the Quran. He spoke with a little glint of rebellion flashing in his eyes from time to time, but I could tell that the power at home lay very much with his wife, and that Fatima's husband knew he was a fortunate man to have married such a formidable woman.

I stayed the night with them and left the next morning, feeling like I was leaving a new mother behind.

From here to the Khunjerab Pass, I would be cycling pretty much continuously uphill. I would be fighting gravity for the next three weeks.

Playing the viola sometimes feels like a fight against gravity. The instrument can seem long and heavy, and if you don't have your hold balanced just so, the viola can weigh you down. If you have it balanced well, however, gravity helps you, especially your bow, to pull a nutty, rich sound from the instrument. Practice, practice, practice. Nowadays I am a little lazy about practising (well, I am writing a book), but back in my teens and twenties, I practised every day for hours and my viola balance was excellent. Gravity was a great help and seemed to even lift the viola onto my shoulder.

It is such a joy playing an instrument when you feel you can do anything, explore any emotion, describe any sound world with your body. I was viola-fit back then, but it's true, I've let myself go a bit now. One of the pieces I played when I was viola-fit, at my audition to get into the Royal Northern College of Music, was Schumann's Adagio and Allegro in A Flat Major.

A flat is a rich, warm key on the viola. None of the brightness of the open A string is allowed, nor even the D string, so the viola sounds slightly muted, with just the sympathetic vibrations of the G and C strings to support the sound directly. It is the sound of evening drawing in.

Schumann had very few good years available to him, between the ones he spent fighting Clara Wieck's dad for the right to marry his daughter and before his syphilis consumed him. When we think of the brief lives of these composers and the amount of work they left behind, it is rather sobering, isn't it, to think what is possible in forty-six years, in Schumann's case. Or thirty-five in Mozart's, or thirty-one for Schubert. And to think of all the things they had to contend with, health- and money- and love-wise. It makes me realise how much time I must waste.

1849 was one of the few good years for Schumann. He had finally married Clara and they had begun to have a family. Schumann was well known in eastern Germany, and his piano concerto was becoming popular. Things were not perfect, though; he had married the finest pianist of the day and his ego often took a battering, with people at Clara's concerts in Russia asking him if he, too, was a musician. His health was very frail as Robert had nervous attacks, periods of blindness and terrible depression.

The Schumanns had moved to Dresden to give Robert some respite; in the orchestra there Robert had heard a very fine horn player called Lewy. J.R. Lewy was a virtuoso valve horn player from France, and Schubert had already written works for him and this new miracle horn, on which you could now play every semitone in the chromatic scale. No more plumbing on stage, no needing to change bits of the horn to play in a different key, or to put your hand up the horn's bell in a particular way to shape a semitone. The instrument had been liberated and all it needed was composers to write for it; Wagner was in Dresden at the time as well, and you can imagine him and Schumann sitting and marvelling at this new free horn sound. Schumann wrote the Adagio and Allegro for Lewy, but was very kind and made a transcription for viola as well. Thanks Robert.

The adagio is a tricky piece to perform, as its phrase lengths are rather unusual. Often phrases have a natural rise and fall, a predictability and regular form to them, but Schumann's often don't. His music was so irregular for the time that people often shunned it, just as we have the terrible trait of shunning ill-formed humans still today.

Schumann's music in the adagio is chromatic and slightly off-kilter, and seems to ask a perpetual question. Again and again the music rises, sometimes keenly, sometimes in supplication. It is only towards the end of the adagio that the climax gives us an answer, but, again, the answer seems to be doubted and when the end comes we are still there looking around us, not too sure of ourselves. Just like Robert with his terrible self-doubt. The music draws inward and inward, landing on a single point of an E flat stuck out at the end of a peninsula. The piano finally throws the solitary note a lifeline, gathers the E flat up and gives it a new home in an A flat major chord.

The charge of the allegro shakes out any doubts, although it does seem almost brutal. Like somebody who is grinning through clenched teeth, after such a moment of reprieve. Was this Schumann's state of mind at that time? Was life for him, with his decaying mind, a constant series of teeth-gritting denials? My primary school teacher Mrs Turner taught us eight-year-olds that the hardest questions were the simplest ones: Who are you? What is life? When is now? Where are we? Schumann asks these questions all the time in his music. In the allegro he seems to answer something, but I'm not convinced. I reckon he was faking it.

From Abbottabad and Fatima, I arrived at Thakot Bridge and saw the Indus for the first time. I was shocked at how grey the water was, flowing under the bridge, and how violent and determined the river looked. I had always known, right from the beginning of my trip, that this was going to be my most serious cycling test. Did my body by now have enough fitness to propel itself up a road that had taken decades to build, that has certain-death drops of thousands of metres down to the Indus, that goes through villages where men carry Kalashnikovs as nonchalantly as if they are bringing home the shopping, and has three five-thousand-metre passes before you get to descend seventy-five kilometres into China?

There were some days during my journey when I just didn't seem to have as much energy as other days, and this part of the journey up the Karakoram Highway didn't start well. Perhaps it was the quality of my sleep, or my menstrual cycle, or the moon phases, but those first two days cycling up the Indus were really tough. I made barely fifty kilometres progress each day and fell into bed beyond exhausted. The only way I kept going was to grab hold of one of the slow trucks making their way up the route and get pulled along for a while, until my right arm or my nerve gave out. The driver's mate would often spot me and always laughed and gave a thumbs-up. My added weight to their already over-burdened axle didn't make any difference and besides, it would be hard for them to go any slower. And so I cycled, and was pulled, up and up, up towards Chilas, Gilgit and Karimabad, past the base of Rakaposhi, past rope bridges, up and up, up to Nirvana.

They play cricket in Nirvana. One morning I cycled round a corner only to be whacked in the face by a cricket ball. Cricket matches seemed to hold Pakistan together, from the border with Iran to the Karakoram Mountains.

The villages became more and more traditional as I rose with the road. Kids came and ran alongside me, asking for money:

'Please sir, one rupee, my school second class.'

'No, sorry.'

'Please sir, two rupees, my school third class.'

At least they were creative with their maths.

The cricketers pushed me up, away from their game on the road, up to the next meeting with a policeman sitting in a bus station. He waved me over with a smile and played my violin with little skill and much glee.

The people's colouring changed, it became more varied as their genes reflected the different peoples who have moved through this area. I passed ginger-haired, freckled boys, men with Slavic eyes and high cheekbones, dark-skinned people from the very south and, always, the most handsome people in the world, the Pathans.

I saw fewer shops with fancy goods, fewer local cars, more donkeys and men with haggard, toughened faces. Greenery became more and more infrequent, circumscribed by water. As I cycled, the view became like a child's drawing of heaven — blue blue sky, snow-capped mountains, pine trees and waterfalls, orchards and always, at the heart of the scene, the Indus.

An owner of a hotel told me how crops have been grown in the area for centuries, irrigated by water melting from glaciers. As you look up the small valleys coming down into the larger valley of the Indus, you see threads of cultivation descending and joining with the trunk of this giant water tree. When villagers need water in a valley where there is none, they bring ice from a female and male glacier (the owner didn't explain *how* you tell the gender of a glacier), carry them in complete silence and join them in a chosen place to make a new glacier. Silence here, then, is sometimes a necessity.

In one tiny place I stopped at a teashop for a cup of tea. Only men walked the main street and they strolled proudly past, their AK-47s swung over their shoulders. I went inside a wooden shop built over the Indus, and two teenage boys came and sat next to me. They were not as talkative or cheerful as young men further south, but they were as inquisitive. My violin case was at my feet, and they touched it and gestured for me to open it. I did, they saw the instrument and their eyes widened. They looked so hopeful that I would play, and so I gently brought the slow movement from Bach's A Minor Sonata to life. The slow movement is in C major and is a delicate thread of music, rising as the valleys rise from the simple bass. The violin is made to sound like two separate instruments accompanying themselves, as the underneath notes pulse away and the melody sings out on top. It is a simple piece, but tricky to pull off. I thought I had failed these two boys, as I had only got two or three bars into the music when they hushed me with a terrified look on their faces. I immediately realised that it was not my playing that had horrified them, but the very music itself. I was cycling into a land where music, apart from the call to prayer, was banned. Silence, necessary silence.

The British called this area Yaghistan, the land of the ungovernable; central government in Pakistan may well say the same thing these days. Qaleem, the district commissioner from Sukkur, had travelled all the way down the Indus many years ago, and the only place he had had any trouble was here. People shot at him from the riverbank with AK-47s; apparently if these guns are on automatic mode they are not very accurate, and that is the only reason he survived. To the west the Hindu Kush Mountains rise up into the North West Frontier Province; it is here that American drones strike daily, aiming at Al-Qaeda terrorists, but frequently killing civilians.

Why are these people expendable in Americans' minds?

The Karakoram Highway continued north and now east, to the town of Karimabad at about 2500 metres in altitude. Karimabad is at the heart of the Hunza Valley, the truth behind the fable of Shangri-La. I planned to stay here a few days, restock my mind, body and supplies, acclimatise and rest before the final push to the Khunjerab Pass. I was also keen to meet up and hopefully travel with other cyclists who may be going over the pass, as I had heard and read terrifying stories about packs of dogs roaming the high lands leading to the pass and beyond. I was, am, very scared of packs of wild dogs. You may be too. I arrived in the town and camped in the courtyard of a backpacker place, waiting each day for cyclists to arrive. It was August by now, peak cycling season. The Karakoram is the highest paved international road in the world, so quite a few cyclists come to Pakistan just to ride it. A cyclist arrived on my second day, but he was going the wrong way (for me). The news he brought was wrong too: he had been attacked by a pack of dogs as he descended from China and he had only managed to escape from them by hitting them with his pump. This made me even more worried and I wished very, very hard for a knight in shining lycra to turn up the next day and agree to cycle with me.

And one did. Actually two. As I was sitting in the courtyard having a dragon tattooed onto my arm by a German called Peter who had learnt Thai tattooing in the Bangkok 'Hilton', two South African men rolled into the yard on touring bikes and asked for a room. I couldn't have been more relieved, but would they allow me to go with them? And would we be travelling at the same speed?

The tattoo barely dry, I went over to them, introduced myself, gave what I hoped was my most winning smile, asked if they would be my knights and they straight away said yes. They would love to have the company. Their names were Alan and Jason.

We stayed three more days in Karimabad, climbing up to the old Baltit Fort, staying in a village behind the town with a lookout onto the seven-thousand-metre mountains, and being invited by families to visit their houses. We went to one home where the family were drying apricots on the roof, and they honoured us with apricot soup. The people who live in Hunza are some of the best educated in Pakistan and among the healthiest in the world. Their world is clean. The nearest factories are hundreds of kilometres away and the only pollution is from the trucks grinding up and down the highway. The Hunzas' work is physically demanding so they remain strong and active into their nineties and beyond. The diet of the Hunza people is full of nuts, fruit in season, whole grains and little alcohol.

The main religion here is Ismaili Islam, a branch of Shia Islam; the Ismailis' hereditary leader is the Aga Khan. You may remember the Bolan Pass back in the south of Pakistan, and how the British had brought an army through there to fight the first Anglo–Afghan War? Hasan Ali Shah, the forty-sixth Imam of the Ismailis and, thanks to a Persian king, now the first Aga Khan, had helped them. Not only that, he also went on to help the British in Sindh when they captured the province and got to make the Latin pun. So my journey was in some ways a recreation of his journey, although his ended in Mumbai, where he is buried. The British had so much respect for him that in the end they called him 'Your Royal Highness'; nowadays the Aga Khan Foundation provides funds and networks for social and cultural developments around the world, regardless of nationality or religion.

The day came for us three to set off and cycle to the watershed of Asia. The water that drops on top of the Khunjerab Pass will either end up flowing north towards the Taklamakan Desert or south, towards the Indian Ocean. This part of the journey from England to Hong Kong was particularly daunting for me. I was nervous about it, in the same way I would be nervous about an important concert; I didn't want to stuff it up. The thought of crossing three nearly five-thousand-metre passes on a bicycle seemed somehow in the wrong scale. A bicycle was something you rode down to the shops, not over a continental watershed.

I swapped my worn rear tyre with my one remaining spare and set off with my new travelling companions, the Springboks. I was glad I had changed my rear tyre; there is a plant that grows on the Karakoram Highway that spits out tyre-penetrating thorns just in time for cycling season. It is one of God's little conundra, like platypuses and the harmonic scale. We met a

The upper reaches of the Indus, in the Karakorams. I wish I could find a way to capture gradient in a photograph. If you know how, please email me.

cyclist coming down from China who had had sixteen punctures in a single day; Alan suffered three punctures in the first day because his tyres were rubbish. The whole of my trip I only had eight punctures, and six of them were in the last two weeks with emergency Chinese tyres. My choice — Schwalbe Marathon Plus. Use them, or bring a swag of inner tubes and patience.

The fir and fruit trees eventually gave way to high-altitude meadow on the slopes above the road. Down in the Hunza Valley people were growing apricots, almonds, walnuts, pears, peaches, cherries, wheat, millet, mulberries and barley.

As we climbed to the end of Pakistan, we spent one night in a hostel where all the guests slept together in a small room to keep warm. About twenty of us, all travelling in different ways, prepared for bed at the same time, rolled out our sleeping bags and fell together into the dead of night. It was as if we were at a specialist boarding school for travellers, with us cyclists in our grungy uniform of lycra, beanies and fleeces.

Night-time was chilly, but during the day the sun slammed down onto our forearms and necks, scorching them. At some point my Canadian sun hat was blown off in a gust of wind and I just managed to rescue it before a swift Pakistani boy on a bus grabbed it. That hat was my saviour: one day, for some stupid reason, I decided to take it off for the morning. It didn't take long for a massive headache to develop. I wore it continuously for the next two months, but the memory of the sun is still there on my deeply freckled forearms.

We arrived in Sost, the town where you must go through Immigration and Customs before heading up the last seventy kilometres or so to the actual land border with China. The streets were lined with truck drivers, sleeping under their blankets. Alongside the hundreds of drivers taking goods to and from China, we queued up at the outside desks to be stamped out of the country. Our passports would then be checked at various police barriers up the mountain road.

We had to stock up on enough food in Sost to last us for three days until we arrived in Tashkurgan, in China. Eating enough was a continual effort for me by now. If you want to lose weight, cycle up the Karakoram. At the market we loaded up with rice, dried fruit, rice, lentils and more rice. Water was available from the river.

I felt so miserable to leave Pakistan; I had totally fallen in love with these proud people and it was like saying goodbye to a dear, dear friend. Pakistanis had nurtured me through their country and I loved them for it. When people return from Pakistan with bad stories, part of me wonders, what happened? Is it true that we make our own welcome? Certainly some of the Western travellers I had seen, particularly women but also some men, were dressed in rather shocking ways — shorts, tight tops, sleeveless shirts — and behaving as if they were still in their own country, talking loudly and being imperious. Before we start to criticise countries and the experience we have in them, it is maybe good to look at ourselves first. I found that if I went into a place and was tired and therefore not in a particularly good mood, people's attitude towards me was not nearly as friendly.

We cycled out of Sost the next morning as soon as the sun came up, hoping to make it to a police hut where we could camp about ten kilometres below the pass. I was still in Pakistan, but the country felt like it was slipping away as the landscape became more and more desert-like. It was Pakistan according to the map, but the world was changing and a new country was emerging, one of yaks over on the mountainside and ginger, squeaking marmots scurrying to their holes; a country where the bright light shines unimpeded by as much oxygen, a country that is home to some of the highest mountains in the world.

Arriving at the hut before dark was going to be tight, but if we kept a nice steady average speed of fifteen kilometres an hour it should be fine.

We didn't. Perhaps it was me dragging my feet, my pedals, not wanting to leave the country. There were too many spots by the river to stop and make a cup of tea, too many views to marvel at and remember. We spent too long cooking our lunch, chatting and napping until a policeman came over and said we should get going if we were to make it to the hut before sunset. As the sun fell behind the mountains and we spent the last hour cycling in the gloaming along the slate streams by the road, we realised we would have to find a campsite somewhere other than the police hut. The riverbed was dry by now and the best place we could find was away from the road a little, behind a slate mound. We put up our separate tents, cooked rice and fruit and tried to sleep. It was the darkest night, like a velvet chador, and it felt like the mountains on either side were breathing, but at the slowest speed in the universe.

The next morning we made it to the police hut in less than an hour, where they gave us, surprise surprise, a cup of tea. The policemen laughed at us for not arriving the night before, and took a long time checking out our bikes and equipment.

It was now time to engage my final and smallest gear.

Vita has twenty-one gears, three at the front and seven at the back. This is fairly modest compared with contemporary bikes, which have up to thirty gears. The most important thing is the range, not how many gears are in between. Vita's range is wide, a good three octaves, from an ultra-low slow note to a reasonably high, fast one. Not as fast as a racing bike, but Vita isn't a show-off. She is a contralto, not a soprano. Up until now I had managed to avoid using the lowest note, my easiest gear. It seemed comforting to know I had a gear in reserve, something for a rainy day. That rainy day had finally come (actually it was gloriously sunny) and as we pushed off on the final ascent I clicked the gear lever over to number one.

A flat is a key to which Beethoven turned many times, particularly for slow movements of symphonies and concertos in C major or C minor. If he were to follow the classical rules of harmony, for the slow movement he would have gone to the relative major/minor of the main key, or to the dominant, the key a fifth around the circle. But he didn't, and why is that? What does he try to make us feel by going instead a major third lower? You remember his final quartet in F major, when he steps down to D flat for the slow movement? It is the same here, two whole steps down to a subterranean sounding place. And perhaps that is simply it. From a first movement where we stand upright in a key, going a major third down lets us sit and meditate there for a while. There is a real sense of breathing out, rather than breathing in. Think of the first piano concerto. That bravura ending, then a bed of A flat as the orchestra cushions the piano. And the *Pathétique Sonata*'s second movement, also in A flat, coming from a first movement in C. This key of A flat seems to be one of containment, after the vigour and resonance of C. Beethoven's penultimate piano sonata as well, Opus 110, sits in this restrained, gracious key. Beethoven even marks the first movement 'con amabilita', or amiably. Chopin's most used key was A flat. Much of Chopin's music seems to be sad, despite being in a major key, and A flat is optimal for that.

Beethoven's Opus 67, otherwise known as his Fifth Symphony, uses A flat in the slow movement. It's not really that slow, marked 'andante con moto', or at a fair walking pace. Since I was just about moving at walking pace, this was a perfect piece to have floating through my head as I cycled up the final kilometres to the Khunjerab Pass. Looking at my cycle computer, it said five kilometres an hour. Alan, one of the Springboks, had decided to really go at a walking pace and actually walk. Although we were ascending so gradually, still the thinner air took its toll on my breathing and I inhaled as deeply as I could, my legs going round ... round ... round. I refused to get off and walk and probably go faster.

And there it was. In the distance, the top of the pass. The other side, China. I watched little streams drip down through the rocks, thinking of their luck flowing to the warmth of the Indian Ocean rather than falling over the other side and evaporating in the desert. My nerves finally dissipated; we had done it, we had cycled to the watershed of Asia, and soon the most glorious of rewards, a downhill freewheel for seventy-five kilometres.

Our passports were checked one last time and I shook the hand of my final policeman. Amir the army major had warned me about the police all those weeks ago, but, apart from the initial problem in Sibi, I had found them to be totally delightful. They had sheltered me from crowds in their police stations, they had put me up, they had given me tea before sunrise and they had admired my sturdy thighs. I would have to write to Amir to tell him.

Leaving a country seems to distil your feelings about it into that moment. There have been countries (I'll leave it to your imagination) I was so pleased to leave that I've smiled as I passed through Immigration. Others where I was left a little unaffected. But this time tears sprang into my eyes as I shook the policeman's hand. I tried to be Pakistani about it and be bold and proud. I was going to miss that crowd.

We sat at the top for a while, made a cup of tea and talked to musicians from a Chinese Tajik delegation who were going to give concerts down on the plain, five kilometres in altitude below. After an hour it was time to get going; it was getting chilly and we still had two days of cycling before we got to Tashkurgan. I turned back for a final look at Pakistan and waved to my friends back on the plains — in Quetta, in Sukkur, in Lahore, in police stations, army barracks, teashops and beside the road for over two thousand kilometres. And, once again, I stepped into a new country.

E flat major/minor

The number of kebabs that a man can eat in a day, when he is from a country that eats a lot of meat and he hasn't had any for three days, will never cease to astound me.

The Springboks ate one hundred kebabs between them, over two days, when we arrived in Tashkurgan. I don't think we did anything else other than eat.

The descent of seventy-five kilometres was the most fun I have ever had on a bicycle. It went on for hours, through a landscape that was now extremely dry. Landscapes up to now had had gradual changes, even in the descent from Quetta; this time the severity of the watershed had divided the land, one side blessed with water, and one side with desert. Looking at a map of this part of the world, the borders of Pakistan, Afghanistan, Tajikistan, Kyrgyzstan, India and China seem to crash together, just as these mountains would have done millions of years ago. The Pamir join the Hindu Kush, which join the Karakorams, which join the Himalaya. It is a world of either extreme war, or extreme peace. It is hard to make out which country ends where, apart from the difference in dryness, and you wonder how these borders could ever have been drawn up. As I travelled from England to Hong Kong, the ridiculousness of borders became more and more evident. Borders did not lie on lines, but in people's heads. Someone in an office had drawn these, with no regard to native peoples, or geographical changes. It was like trying to split a violin from a viola. There is some natural overlap, which is to be celebrated.

The longest descent wasn't without its pains; for days, months, I had been using certain muscles to propel Vita and myself. These muscles were now redundant, thanks to gravity, and new, less-used ones came into play: shoulder muscles and biceps to keep Vita from hitting potholes, static thigh muscles for coming up out of the seat to save my arse from vibrating off with the roughness of the road, and neck muscles to isolate my head from the shaking. Vita has no suspension (well she is a big toughie) and that was the single day I slightly missed it. Suspension was just another thing that could go wrong and it is heavy, so I had chosen to keep Vita in her original form as a rigid bike. Aluminium has a little give in it, but if Vita cracked her frame I would be just a bit stuffed trying to find someone to weld her back together again.

She remains whole.

From Tashkurgan, after a day watching a man mix adobe in a bucket to make a house wall, and having Chinese people laugh at the number of kebabs we ate, we cycled through the most exquisite valley towards Kashgar. This place seemed the most remote of the trip, with the Pamir to our left and the Taklamakan Desert to our right. We camped next to goat herders, who invited us in to their tent for sour tea and old biscuits, and we waited patiently on the single-lane road for herders on horses to move their sheep along. And there, all this time, the snow-capped Pamir mountains.

It was time to say goodbye to the Springboks. Alan and Jason were leaving by plane from Kashgar to go to Tibet. We had hung out in Kashgar, gone to the market and bid on a horse (thank heavens we bid low), seen different mosques and cycled through streets where traditional Uygur houses were standing bravely against the Han Chinese onslaught. Those South African men had been perfect knights, and it would be odd to get back to being

Farmers bidding for sheep and horses at the market in Kashgar. If you can, try to go before all the old city is completely destroyed by developers.

solitary again. As a trio I had noticed a difference in how we were treated: people stood back a little and took more time to start talking to us. I was keen to take away the barrier of a group from travelling, to get back to a simple contact with people.

Kashgar was beautiful in 2000, but I wonder how it is now. There was much talk about how the majority Han Chinese were going to tear down all the old buildings and rebuild using glitzy, shiny materials rather than mud and stone. As I made my way through China, I would become more and more appalled by the generic architecture. In an equivalent in music, it would be like only ever having two chords in a piece. There are show buildings like opera houses and skyscrapers in big cities that are magnificent and fascinating and add more interest, but in the smaller cities — ones of just a few million people as opposed to mega cities of twenty million — the repetition of the architecture is mind-numbing, brainwashing and extremely depressing.

If you look at a map of this western part of China you will see an enormous empty space. No towns, no roads, no woods, no rivers. This is the Tarim Basin and the Taklamakan Desert. My big decision now was whether to attempt to cycle around this three-thousand-kilometre-wide dry land, or take the bus.

I had met a few cyclists coming from Kashgar who had cycled through China.

'Did you cycle across the Taklamakan?'

'No,' they always said. Either because the distances were too far between towns, they had heard the roads were very bad or that the wind (the biggest enemy or friend of the cyclist) would be against them the whole way.

I bought the best map I could find in Kashgar, the largest scale, to attempt to decipher this enormous space. Taklamakan means various possible things: abandoned place; a place you can enter but not leave; the sea of death. You are probably getting the picture that it is an extremely extreme place of, um, extremities. Come to think of it, what desert isn't? But it is also home to a large section of the Silk Road, and for that reason I wanted to cycle it. I wouldn't be on a camel, but at least if I were cycling, I wouldn't be on a bus. I scoured the map, looking for clues. There were some: hopeful little white dots where towns or villages might be, about one hundred and fifty kilometres apart. The road seemed to be flat (good), but then exposed to winds (maybe bad). The state of the road from the border to Kashgar didn't really give me much cause for hope of a smooth ride.

Learning what you can from maps is an endlessly fascinating activity — the initial action of unfolding the map and opening it onto your lap or a table, then smelling and feeling the stiff paper as it falls over the edges of the support, the moment of putting your mind inside that map and arousing your adventure taste buds. (To fold it up again in the same way is another matter.) Then your eye starts to scan roads, mountains, rivers, looking for somewhere new to go, for a place that has 'adventure' ringing it invisibly. Maps are such a mixture of potential and fact. I love that to read a map accurately, you must use your imagination in a very specific way.

One Sunday a few years ago I was at a loose end and unfolded a map of northern India and the Himalayas onto the kitchen table. A road caught my eye, one that followed the Ganges and the Alaknanda Rivers to their source around Govindghat, close to Tibet and Nepal. Follow a little thin line from there and you come upon the Valley of Flowers. The map I was looking at made it very clear, with a great big red star, that this was a place of huge beauty and significance, but if I hadn't been led there by the lure of the river road I would have missed it. I ended up having a magnificent two weeks cycling up this road alongside thousands of Sikhs in buses and jeeps, them going to their holy place, me to mine. It was Sikh holy season, but the map hadn't told me that. Maps can give you deep information, but it is tempting to be so involved in the map that you miss where you really are. One time I had been driving my mum around Italy. Mum doesn't drive, but is an excellent navigator who needs to know where she is on a map. We were not quite sure at that moment, but there was an exquisite, quintessentially Tuscan view from the window.

'Aha!' said Mum. 'We are here!' pointing at the map.

'No, Mum, we're here!' I said, pointing at the view.

Sheet music is a map of music. It tells you the route through the piece, where to go up and down, even what speed to go, but it doesn't tell you where the heart of the music is, where the truth of the music lies. Simply being able to read music does not make you a musician. And so it was with reading the map of the Taklamakan. I could read it, I could study it, but I couldn't tell where the heart of that desert was and whether I would be able to cross it or not. Indeed, how my heart was.

I decided to give it a go. I would hate to not be brave, then halfway there on a bus realise that the roads were excellent, there were petrol stations and lovely little hotels all the way along and the wind would be behind me.

In my basic Mandarin, I asked everybody I could about the road. They all shook their heads.

Learning a musical instrument is a fine balance between playing pieces that are challenging enough for you so that you develop, and not so challenging that you give up. When I was about fourteen my viola teacher Mr Stace had decided to give me some Brahms, his viola sonata in E flat. Oh, okay, his clarinet sonata, which he then transcribed for viola because he thought it would sound better (clarinetists and viola players always have a little scrap over this). This was the first big grown-up piece I had played, apart from the Bach Cello Suites, and when I looked at the map of the music I was terrified. That very same sheet music that terrified me then is in my hands now, over thirty years old, frayed, worn, stained, broken, loved. The palimpsest of rubbings-out and rewritings of bowing, fingering and phrasing is there on the yellowing pages. The sheet music is no longer whole. The first movement page turn was made so many times that the join is broken; I have to gingerly turn the single sheet and readjust it next to the others. As I practised this piece over the years, making it as flawless as I could, the map of it gradually gave way.

But this first time I gazed at the music of Brahms, there were so many new things to look at; this was a whole new world of phrase markings that disguised themselves as slurs, new, frequent tempo changes, the equivalent of contour lines as the notes swept up and down the viola, and cadences that acted like junctions in the music. As I would with the map of the Taklamakan, I spent a long time just looking at the music manuscript, reading it, trying to find where the heart of the music was.

There is no substitute for doing, though; eventually I played the music and eventually I cycled into the desert. The Brahms became familiar and comfortable after hours of exploring; I could only trust the desert would do the same.

I had dipped a toe into the sands of the desert by leaving Kashgar and cycling northeast, to Kizilsu. One limitation to travelling and stopping in small towns in China is that foreigners are not allowed to stay in just any old hotel. They have to go to government-approved ones, and then are obliged to pay a higher rate. It was hard finding a hotel that would accept me in Kizilsu, and it was only going to get more difficult.

The next morning I headed out to cycle more than one hundred kilometres to the next little white dot, which may or may not have somewhere to stay. I still had my tent, but frankly I would rather not camp. To the northwest the Tian Shan Mountains stood as a barrier to Kyrgyzstan, to the south the Taklamakan lay as a barrier to life. Tian Shan means 'heavenly mountain', so I was cycling between heaven and hell.

The white dots proved quite accurate. Around one hundred and twenty kilometres from Kizilsu a reluctance of buildings slouched by the road, one of them a truck drivers' stop. I cycled into the yard and asked for a room, in my most winning Mandarin. Amazingly the manager didn't blink an eye and showed me to a small, clean room with the most wonderfully heavy doona on the bed. It felt like an entire flock of sheep had donated their coats to make that doona. There was even a rudimentary bathroom with hot water out the back, so I scrubbed up and went out to find some food. I was starving. I had eaten biscuits all day so I was ready for noodles, rice, anything that didn't crumble. The food stall I ate at served one thing, and one thing alone. I was to realise this dish would be the only thing I would eat, outside of restaurants in towns, for the next three weeks.

The dish is the perfect cyclist's meal: thick wheat noodles cooked with tomatoes, peppers, cabbage and enough garlic to keep every single vampire in the world at bay, topped with mutton. It was utterly delicious. I can still taste it now, which is not surprising as I ate it three, sometimes four times a day. And to wash it down tea made from a large handful of twigs shoved in a bowl with hot water over the top. I never did find out which plant those twigs came from, but that food and tea propelled me onwards around the top of the desert, and I was *so* glad I had decided to be bold, to cycle across the Taklamakan.

There were tough days. It wasn't all easy-peasy and the wind behind me. The road generally was good, but there were some jagged stretches, and the wind often came, laid an arm across my chest and tried to drag me backwards. If I could catch up with them I tried to cycle as close as possible behind trucks, using them as a windbreak. Effective and ridiculously dangerous. The endlessness of the ride began to affect me after a few days, and the relentlessness of it too. I just had to keep going. There was nowhere to hang out for a few days and have a nice coffee and chill. The truck stop managers let me stay for one night, but two would have been out of the question, as the police would find out and fine us both.

One day, somewhere in the middle of this epic, I thought I must have been on my own for too long, as I could swear I was seeing a female, white cyclist coming right towards me. I narrowed my eyes to reduce the glare and there, now stopped by the roadside, was a British cyclist, going to Pakistan. Sarah was about my age, travelling on her own. We made tea and conversation right there, in the hills of the desert, thousands of miles from Britain. It was an extraordinary meeting of women inspired by people like Dervla Murphy and Anne Mustoe, but we were both so intent on our goals that we continued in our own directions. I do regret that, not spending more time celebrating the luck of our meeting. I was too focused on the destination and again forgot the importance of the here and now. I never saw her again.

That night I was mistaken for a man again and propositioned by the female manager of the truck stop. She came and sat on my bed, shirt undone.

All those kilometres cycled, yet on the map it looked like I had hardly moved. I had a minidisc player with me (remember them?) and I rationed out the music to an hour a day, so that I didn't wear it out. You know that thing of wearing out a memory or a picture? I think that can happen with music as well, it loses its effectiveness. I had a bit of pop music on the minidiscs, some Joni Mitchell and Des'ree and some Craig David, but when I really wanted a big lift I stuck on Elgar's *Pomp and Circumstance March No. 1.* I am a little embarrassed to say that, but it is *such* good music, despite the jingoism. Every afternoon around four o'clock, somewhere between Kashgar and Lanzhou, you would have seen a solitary cyclist going along a distant road, hands off the handlebars and conducting an invisible orchestra. A daily Last Night of the Proms in the desert.

All this time and distance did wonderful things for my head too. The final bits of negativity in my life before the bike trip began to fall by the wayside. One thing my dad had said to me before I went was to be mindful that I would come back a different person. And I felt I *was* changing. I think I started to like myself a bit more. Because of the constant, consistent cycling I now had to do my mind started to relax, as it was less distracted by towns and people. During the day I was often the only person on the road for dozens of kilometres at a time; the ride became a long meditation.

The end of the trip would come so soon now, though; I was in my penultimate country and if I kept to schedule I would be in Hong Kong in about two months. I had planned to have about a month back in England, and then begin the adventure of finding a new career. I began to loosely think about media, then, specifically, radio.

When my student quartet began to do regular concerts, I was the one who stood up at the beginning and talked about the music. I spoke to audiences in churches and small halls around the north of England, as we became journeymen of our trade

— the travelling quartet. I had come to know when I could be playful with the audience and when I needed to be serious, when a little fact could lift the enjoyment of a piece and when a question asked could be more revealing of the music. As I cycled through the desert, my mind opened and I remembered this time. I remembered being really happy speaking, happier than actually playing. So maybe radio could be something to try. There was a radio station in Hong Kong that played classical music, RTHK Radio 4, so perhaps I could go and speak to them? Years of drinking whisky and smoking Camels had at least given me a low voice.

I now had a vague career direction, but what about an instrument? This endless, tormenting question. I loved playing my little three-quarter size violin, I loved journeying through Bach's solo sonatas as I journeyed across Europe and Asia. I loved the viola, but I had wanted to try the cello for so many years. I was doing a cycle trip that I hadn't believed would be possible; why not then play the instrument I had never thought possible?

It was time to take charge of my own musical destiny. Just because my mother had put me down for what I considered to be the wrong instrument when I was eight, didn't mean that now, at thirty-three, I shouldn't play the right instrument. If I started now, I thought, in ten years' time maybe I would be okay.

To move forward, we need to make decisions. Whether they are right or wrong.

* * *

Bach wrote six cello suites. Or did he? It has been proposed that Bach's wife, Anna Magdalena, composed the cello suites; there are no surviving manuscripts except the fifth suite in Johann's hand, only in Anna's, and the music is considered relatively simplistic for him to have written. Johann was a young man when the suites were written; he was working for a prince in Anhalt-Cöthen who loved music for its own sake, not just for its use in religious services, and he encouraged Bach to write secular works for the other fine musicians the duke employed. And so it is that on our CD shelves today and in our computers sit the exceptional solo works by Bach for cello and violin. The viola plays them all, but there is one work I feel works so much better on the cello than the viola, and that is the fourth suite in E flat.

The fourth suite is probably best recognised by its Prelude. You can imagine it as an organ piece, with a low bass note resounding under a simple broken arpeggio of the chord, then moving to another chord in the next bar, each change momentous. Music to be played with feet as well as hands. The suite has echoes of the first in the way it moves with a repetitive pattern from chord to chord. The difference is that the first prelude's pattern goes up and stays there; in the fourth prelude the pattern is constantly falling, like an Escher drawing. This prelude is punctuated by virtuosic flourishes of toccata-like notes and the pattern is less smooth, more granular, as the notes march through the instrument. The first prelude glides, this one stamps. I played this suite on the viola for my college diploma at the Northern, and although I gave it my best shot and got a pretty good mark, still I have never been able to create enough hugeness or weight with it; not necessarily volume, but resonance. I would hear cellists play it and some, like Rostropovich and Tortelier, played it how I imagined it, but no matter how hard I tried it just wasn't happening on my viola.

The trick is to have the bass note sustain as long as possible throughout the bar. This is not a problem when the bass note is an open string, but when it is a stopped note, especially if that note does not ring particularly with the other open strings, then the piece can sound too dry. Playing it in a church makes things easier and that's probably the place for which Bach wrote it, not for a slightly arid concert hall. Or a desert.

The prelude has many difficulties and delights, continuing through the rest of the suite. These suites are like little European Unions of music — allemandes from Germany, correntes from Italy, minuets from France and gigues from England. And the slowest movement, the sarabande, from Spain.

The sarabande's map, its manuscript, is one of an open plain with regular features and no obvious hazards. By Bach's time the sarabande was heard as a graceful, rather noble and refined dance, but travel back in time nearly two hundred years from J.S. and you would have been arrested if you danced it. Just as Frankie Goes to Hollywood was banned in the twentieth century and music as a whole is banned in some countries now, the sarabande was banned in Spain in the 1500s because it was too suggestive, too erotic, too blatantly sexual. The innuendo is rather subtle in this music, but there *is* a musical conundrum: a sarabande has its stress on the second of the three beats in a bar, but Bach confuses the performer by including a chord, often used as a natural stress, on the *first* beat of the bar. It takes a strong will to avoid making this the focus of the phrase and instead to use the chord as a stepping stone to the resolve of the second beat. As a result the piece has a constant strain and throb to it. Maybe that eroticism is still there after all.

I started playing the cello when I was thirty-four.

A friend lent me her son's Chinese cello; I felt like I was eight again, playing a bright orange, tinny instrument and making a crude sound. I had beginner lessons with my friend Shelagh and played Bach minuets and Breval sonatas; my friends deserted the house while I practised my scales and arpeggios; I obsessed about the cello and bought books, watched videos, went to concerts and angled myself with a perfect line of vision to the cellist; I studied as much as I had time for to win back the years, to squeeze my ten thousand hours into as short a time as possible, and try to become a belated cellist. I moved on to Tim Franks as a teacher; Tim is a beautiful player in the Hong Kong Philharmonic who did the best thing any teacher can do — encouraged me. I took my grade five within six months and my grade eight in a year. I received a better mark than I did on the viola. My viola was left now, abandoned, as I decided to stop playing it completely to give my hand a chance to change shape in how it stretched. As I planned to emigrate from Hong Kong to Australia in 2002, Tim encouraged me to apply for a postgraduate place at the Victorian College of the Arts in Melbourne. I was doubtful. Who would choose such a new cellist for a postgraduate course? I went ahead and made a videotape of myself playing the Shostakovich sonata and wrote a letter describing my perhaps unusual journey and subsequent gap between technical ability and musical intentions. Tony Gould, then Dean of Music, welcomed me; I couldn't believe it. Maybe this interrupted cadence was going to work out; maybe I could become a cellist.

Cadence on a bicycle is a vitally important thing. Turn your pedals too slowly, with too hard a gear, and you wear out your muscles and your chain. The trick is to have a light, quick cadence, an allegro cadence, not andante, one where your lungs do the heavy work and your muscles hardly have to strain at all. This is how Pantani and Armstrong cycled up the twenty-one switchbacks of the Alpe d'Huez, so fast they had to brake on the corners. I decided to try and copy them in this brisk style; the EPO and human growth hormone were a bit hard to obtain in the Taklamakan, though.

Once you have trained your body to have a swifter cadence, cycling becomes something you can do all day. At first it feels shallow, as if you should be experiencing cycling more deeply than this in your legs. Rocking and bouncing on the saddle can also be an issue, as you have to learn to stabilise your body with your core and make a smoother stroke. As one leg pushes down, the other lifts and pulls up (if you are using cleats). You need to cycle with your heart as well as your body, like playing an instrument; indeed after a while cycling becomes like dancing, or painting. One of the most beautiful things I ever heard said by an athlete was Ian Thorpe commenting how, for him, swimming was more like art than sport. After all these thousands of kilometres, I was beginning to have the smallest inkling of what he meant. One day I was so in the zone with Vita, the road was so smooth and the wind so kind that I cycled two hundred and seventy kilometres in a day. As I swung my leg over the saddle to get off at the end, I was in a completely altered state; as a sailor has sea legs, I had bicycle legs, still spinning as I walked into a truck stop.

My map showed the distance I had come after two weeks; I had nearly made it to Jiayuguan, the most westerly point of the Great Wall of China, historically the place where Chinese people were exiled to the West through a single narrow gate. Once past Jiayuguan, I would be well clear of the Tarim Basin and the Taklamakan Desert. There was one big hurdle in my way: between two white dots was a distance of three hundred kilometres. Even if all the conditions were heavily in my favour, this would be too much to cycle. I decided to be brave and camp halfway in the desert.

I stocked up with rice and biscuits and headed out as early as I could; the country was like a desiccated hilly Shropshire now, with all the green sucked away and turned to pale brown. As my legs turned the pedals and the pedals turned the cranks and the cranks turned the chain and the chain turned the sprocket and the sprocket turned the wheel, it seemed like I was simply along for the ride, making virtually no effort. I had finally done my ten thousand hours.

A man on a motorbike came up behind me, wanting to chat. There were so few cars on the road, just trucks really, and virtually no motorbikes (in fact I had seen more camels than motorbikes), so I was surprised to see him. He may well have been surprised to see me. It was getting to the end of the afternoon by now and I had just begun scouting for somewhere to camp. All this time, and I still hadn't got up the nerve to camp in the wild on my own. This may well be my last chance on this trip.

I chatted a little bit to motorbike man; normally this would go on for a few sentences in my bad Mandarin, they would get bored/have gleaned what information they wanted, and then they would drive off. This time that didn't happen.

Motorbike man had an uneasy manner and began to ask me where I was staying the night. I knew that he knew there was nowhere within cycling distance. There wasn't the same level of threat from him as there had been from the man in Iran, but still, my chance of camping in the desert was blown. There was no way I could escape him and leave the road unseen. I had to give up, and hitch a ride on a truck for the final hundred kilometres.

Don't be afraid to give up.

Some days I hated playing the cello. I hated the way my left hand felt, having to stretch at a different angle and never seeming as fluid as it did on the viola. I hated my slow learning and out-of-tune playing and the feeling of never being at home with the instrument. I hated the way my right thumb hurt from pressing too hard with the bow. I began to think I had made a terrible mistake and would be forever trapped in a no-man's-land of music — knowing what I wanted to hear, but never being skilled enough to produce it, like a dream where you want to scream then realise you have no mouth.

Playing with other musicians led me away from this dead-end thinking. Why play an instrument, if all you are ever going to do is judge yourself and compare yourself with others? Fred Riddle, the principal viola player of the London Symphony Orchestra when they were in *Star Wars* prime, taught me that there is no point comparing yourself to others; there will always be somebody better, louder, faster and more musical than you; all you can do is play for yourself. This slowly sank into my mind as I began to play the cello in quartets, sometimes for paid gigs, more often for simple delight.

I started to get up at 5.30am to practise before work. My neighbours were remarkably kind (or deaf) as I played exercises for two hours, in the dark of a Melbourne winter. By now I was studying privately with Philip Green, and he had given me new hope that I might one day be, for me, an acceptable cellist.

I had bought a beautiful cello in Hong Kong, a copy of a Gagliano (copy everything in Hong Kong), but my bow was rubbish and I needed a new one.

I started looking for a better bow and visited a magical instrument shop on Bridge Road in Richmond. The Violineri isn't there any more (try Box Hill now), but for many years people would walk just that little further up the road than they needed to, simply to gaze through the window at a man who looked like Father Christmas and who worked with strange tools, repairing the souls of violins, violas and cellos. From the street, with buses and trams and cars and all the sounds of the twenty-first century whizzing past, you could see bits of instruments that in a slightly different form had been making sounds for the last millennium.

Bows are as important as the instrument. The design of instruments has hardly changed in hundreds of years, but bows have changed quite significantly, from a convex shape with the horsehair tied to the end and tightened with your hand, to a concave shape, with the hair tightened with a screw mechanism and much more tension in the stick. Today's bows have the power to deliver a bigger sound for the modern concert hall and are decorated with gold, silver, mother-of-pearl, even mammoth ivory. They are generally made from pernambuco, a wood that is only grown in Brazil, but now the harvesting of the tree is banned, so bow makers are turning to different materials — snake wood, carbon fibre.

The difference a bow makes was most clearly demonstrated to me by Samir, in Kabul.

Samir at the time, 2013, was seventeen, a graceful, long-legged chap who played the violin well, but who dreamt of playing the viola. I taught him a few times at the Music Institute, and when Samir played my viola, he sounded like he had been playing for decades, not five minutes. We were preparing for concerts in Kabul, and then Samir and the Afghan Youth

Samir the elegant violinist. Samir was always keen to learn and stayed behind after school to spend more time practising with me. He has huge talent and a great sense of humour.

Orchestra were going on an historic first tour to the USA, where they would play in the most famous concert hall in the world, Carnegie Hall. Isaac Stern and others had saved the hall from demolition in the sixties. When asked how you get to Carnegie Hall, Stern had replied, 'Practice, practice, practice.' Samir was going to Carnegie Hall within a month and, even better, he was going to play with Isaac Stern's own bow within five minutes.

Mikhail Simonyan, a Russian violin soloist, came into our practice room. Mischa was going on tour with the Afghans and was also teaching for a few weeks before. As he is such a magnificent violinist, he has the choice of violins belonging to various trusts for him to play. Only the richest soloists can afford to buy their own Stradivarius/Guarneri/eighteenth-century instrument, so the rest have to borrow ones from charities and societies and banks. Mischa played on Nathan Milstein's Stradivarius, on loan, with Isaac Stern's Pajeot bow; this was about the best combination you could have. Mischa had left the Strad at home, but Stern's bow had come to Kabul.

Samir and I were working on a tricky little passage in Vivaldi's *Four Seasons*. Samir's problem was nothing to do with his own ability; it was entirely to do with his rubbish bow. He was trying to get a clear sound, but because his bow was so slack and woolly he kept slowing down. He could either play clearly and slowly, or muddily and quickly. Nobody, not even Mischa, could make a decent sound with Samir's bow.

We tried the passage a few times, gradually getting quicker, but with not a lot of success. Then Mischa threw out an invitation that Samir will probably never forget:

'Here, try Stern's bow.'

Samir at this point had no idea who Isaac Stern was. He took the bow from Mischa's hand, tenderly wrapped his fingers around the frog, and played.

I suspect it was the best sound Samir had ever made on the violin. He played the Vivaldi with Mischa, me recording the moment for radio. The clarity of Samir's sound, the distinction of each note was simply superb. They reached the end of the passage and Mischa burst out laughing with the delight of a child. Isaac Stern's bow had made it to Kabul, a young Afghan had used it and it had massively improved his playing. Isaac Stern would have been very, very pleased.

* * *

In the violin shop on Bridge Road, I found three things: a bow, a friend and a quartet.

I walked into the shop and the smells of varnish and rosin bounced into my nose; the same smells, the same tools, the same designs that have been used for around five hundred years. There was nothing in that shop that needed electricity to make it work.

It is tempting to think of such places as anachronistic, but they aren't, really. It's just that they are rare. If you ever see such a place, go in. It is a little gift for the soul.

The bow I found was made by Herr Wanker (thank heavens he is German) and I fell in love with it straight away. Perhaps the best way to describe how to choose a bow is to simply say that, like wands in Harry Potter, the bow seems to choose you. As soon I played with this bow, I knew I would never need another; its weight melted into my palm and it seemed as if I had an extra ten years' practice up my sleeves, it made playing so much more facile. And it was tipped with woolly mammoth too.

The friend and the quartet came together; the owner of the shop is an octogenarian viola player called Brenton Fyfield, the Father Christmas lookalike. Brenton stood in his shop behind a massive wooden workbench, strewn with shavings, bits of violins, pencils, callipers, gouges, chisels and pots of glue. He wore a thick apron and an even thicker white beard, with some of the wood shavings stuck in it. He wore sandals and his toenails were painted different colours. His body was stooped over a tiny violin, split open, in the middle of surgery. The sounds of Bridge Road were shut out as the door jangled closed behind me and, as he looked up, this magical instrument man entranced me completely.

After trying out a few bows and eventually finding my Wanker, Brenton asked me if I would like to play some quartets with him, his wife Miranda and his wife's son Martin. In the years since I had been asked the same thing at music college I had learnt to trust my instincts, so instead of hesitating and saying I would get back to him, I immediately said yes please. I couldn't pass up the chance to play with an eighty-year-old, a sixty-year-old and a twenty-year-old.

As we played together over the following months, the depth of Brenton's musical knowledge was slowly revealed to me. And no wonder; he has been playing the violin and viola since he was nine years old.

Brenton's dad was an English sailor who came to Australia at the beginning of the twentieth century. Brenton's mum was a school teacher. In Ballarat, back around the time of the Second World War, the common thing to do was to leave school early and get a job, so that is what Brenton did. In 1946 he left behind school and the hope of going to a conservatoire and took a job in an office. He was fifteen.

From there Brenton worked as a book-keeper and eventually a legal clerk. He married and had three children, which he calls his dry period, but all the while he played the violin and viola, drove himself hundreds of kilometres for lessons and played chamber music with whomever he could find.

Brenton began to teach himself to fix violins, to become a luthier. The best way he could think of to do this was to take instruments apart to see how they were built, so that's exactly what he did. Starting with cheap Chinese instruments, he eventually moved on to older, dearer ones; Brenton slowly transformed himself from a clerk into a luthier.

Although Brenton's path wasn't easy, he eventually did what he had wanted to do from the age of twelve or so — play with string instruments. He now runs one of the most successful and longest-running repair shops in Victoria and still practises his scales at eighty-three years old. Brenton has been playing the violin for nearly seventy-five years.

And we have been playing together ever since that first meeting. Geography gets in the way now, but for a few years we would meet every Monday in Scotchmer Street, North Fitzroy, and saunter and skip through Mozart and early Beethoven (a bit easier). Haydn remains our speciality though. We are not blessed with the best intonation, but we do play with great spirit and have managed to get to the end of a few quartets without either bursting out laughing or getting lost. Our favourite things to have among our music stands are Gyp the dog and a bottle of red. We have performed in private houses, the Melbourne Recital Centre and a tractor shed. The shed had a particularly fine acoustic.

Playing in this quartet taught me the bliss of playing the cello and being the bass. The ecstasy of being at the root of the harmony changes and playing the bass notes from which the second violin and viola would bounce off, the exhilaration of being the motor for the speed, the gratification of producing a sound that provided a bed for the other three instruments; it was everything I had hoped it would be, it was more than I could have imagined, it was what I had fantasised about when I was eight years old.

* * *

I arrived in Lanzhou in October, ready for a good hotel and something that wasn't noodles to eat. I found both, and was discreetly followed by a 'taxi driver' (a policeman?) for two days as I walked around the town. As I still needed to occasionally escape from the here and now, I bought *War and Peace*, continuing on from *Anna Karenina*, and went map shopping. Despite my eager search, still the best map seemed to be the one I had found in London, small scale, but clear, with Roman and Chinese script, and with minor roads marked as well. It was beginning to show the wear of being used, just as the Brahms sonata has.

After a few days' rest, I headed south and, for the first time for months, a little west, to the Tibetan Autonomous Region town of Xiahe.

As I climbed out of the Lanzhou valley, autumn was dripping its colourful death through the trees. For a long time I sat and watched a man plough his field with a camel, instead of a buffalo. He looked up, waved and carried on. There was no more interaction necessary for him.

I cycled past roadside markets selling hard cheese and various fermented products and, as the road gently entered the sky, I saw Buddhist monasteries in folds of hills, and pigs being slaughtered by the roadside. The quiet of the desert had gone and the quiet of the Tibetan grasslands had replaced it. Softer, more forgiving, a hush rather than a sshh. Tibetan horsemen stared at me with no embarrassment; I suppose if a Tibetan horseman arrived in my town, I would probably stare at them unashamedly too.

This area, in Gansu Province, is the part of China the government has allowed to remain the most Tibetan. In actual Tibet, the Han Chinese have taken over everything, but here, at least in the year 2000, there was still a strong sense of Tibetanness, and an even stronger smell of fermented butter. Yes I tried it; it's gross.

From Xiahe I cycled higher and higher, out of the valleys and across the grasslands. In one village I stayed a few days to allow my feet to warm up (a perennial cyclist's problem) and was invited by the hotel owner to watch the sky burial of a man in his thirties.

The body was carried up to the mountainside above the village, and immediately a flock of vultures appeared in the sky across the wide valley. Their massive wings and long necks were unmistakable, even from only seeing them in cartoons. In the appointed place, the body was stripped and the man's clothes left to rot with piles of others from years of burials. Tibetan long coats, fur-lined hats, split boots. I sat and looked on this wardrobe of extinction, and the vultures, twenty or so, landed beside the body. They waited, a single jiggling mass, as the body was prepared. It struck me how polite the vultures were, almost as if they were putting on their bibs before a dainty snack.

The undertakers' job in almost-Tibet is very different from one in the West: in the West a body is made presentable and pumped full of preservative; in Tibet the body is destroyed, slashed open to help the vultures eat every single bit. And when the bones have been stripped and cleaned of their marrow, the undertakers smash the skull to make available the brains. It is clean, swift and extraordinarily beautiful to watch. Something to die for.

I had tried to sell my viola in the years since I had begun the cello, but nobody wanted to buy it. Jane, my beautiful, wise partner, advised me to keep it.

'It's been such a part of you for so long, there are so many thousands of shared hours, you can't sell it. And you never know, you might want to play it again, sometime.'

I took my viola out of his case last year, to practise in anticipation of teaching viola in Kabul. I had decided to teach the viola only because the cello was too expensive to take on the plane.

I was scared how I might sound after so long; I had played very rarely in the previous ten years, only to check if my viola was still alive. He was, but barely. Instruments, like humans, retreat into themselves when they are not played and my viola had become quieter and thinner. The water of scales and studies reconstituted my muscle memory of all those thousands of hours of practice as a child. I was amazed how, even after not playing for so long, I could play through whole Bach suites from memory. Just like riding a bike. The years of struggling with the cello seemed cruelly disproportionate to the speed with which I regained my viola chops. Not quite to the standard of my Berlin days, but not too shabby. I felt the unspeakable happiness of meeting a childhood friend again and re-experiencing that deep love.

In the months before I was due to go to Kabul, officials and news reports warned about the dangers there; I began to doubt whether it was really wise to go. By now I was all primed for adventure, though, so I started hunting around for another place to take my viola.

Back a couple of years ago I had seen a documentary about kids from a slum in Mumbai who had performed the *Sound of Music* in a concert hall with the Bombay Chamber Orchestra.

The Bombay Chamber Orchestra. There had to be a musical adventure there.

It turned out that they would be giving a fiftieth anniversary concert in Mumbai in December, so I wrote an email to the founder, Jini Dinshaw, another eighty-year-old viola player. I asked if I could come and interview her and them and, by the way, I also played the viola.

Jini wrote straight back. Yes, of course, and they would love to have me play with them as well. A suitably celebratory program of Rossini, Bizet, Rachmaninov and Rimsky-Korsakov. Even saying those names is fun.

I practised with even more vigour; I returned to the exercises I had done for all those hours in Berlin, found my Rode and Dont studies (the computer wants to turn that into Don't, and I often do too) and began to rediscover my viola centre. My viola woke up as I did, and I started to realise my sound and approach to playing were quite different from BC (Before Cello). Now, with all those years of richness ringing in my ears, my viola sound was becoming fuller, almost swankier. I cared less about trying to make a piece perfect, and more about trying to play it how I wanted it to feel. I began to play the viola how *I* wanted to play.

I travelled to Mumbai in December, as the winter was supposed to be approaching. It was still sweltering, but that didn't deter me from buying an Indian-made Hero bike and cycling round the city and to rehearsals. The bike proudly stated on its frame:

EXTRA DURABLE AND SHINING

Hero remained reasonably shiny, but the cotter pin on his left crank was remarkably non-durable. As I weaved my way back to the breezy relief of Marine Drive through the shiny Mercedes, filthy buses and time-travel Ambassador taxis, a vehement, forte squeak came from the crank. The pedal wobbled at each turn. A slow cadence was going to be in order in India.

The rehearsal for the gala concert was held at a girls' school near Flora Fountain, in the Victorian Gothic part of town. Because many of the members of the BCO worked in other jobs, the orchestra met early and was finished by 8.30am. Then the brass players could return to the police force, the bassoonist to his advertising agency, violinists to their teaching, the cellists to their studies.

I introduced myself to Jini. I'd seen her walking along, a tiny fruit of humanity with thick grey hair and eyes that didn't just twinkle, they gleamed. Jini lived around the corner in the flat where she had been born, and marched round to the school with her Nepalese manservant behind, carrying her viola and a cello.

The orchestra's sound in that first rehearsal was a little chaotic, but miraculous nonetheless. Apart from the string players, most of whom had been taught by Jini, all the others had essentially taught themselves. Jini had pointed them in the right direction to get started and about once a year musicians from England came out and gave masterclasses. These Indian musicians were playing at an inspiring standard, often with a single reed to last them a year.

Jini invited me around to her flat the next day, so that I could interview her for the radio documentary I was making. I walked up to the fifth floor and rang the bell. She promptly opened the door, saying:

'You're on the dot.'

Jini told me, with only the occasional prompt, her life story.

Born into a Parsee family in 1930, she was the youngest of seven children. An orchestra rehearsed in Jini's block of flats, and as a baby she sat on a neighbour's lap, absorbing this sound. Jini's parents never offered her music lessons. All her sisters and her brother learnt piano, singing and violin, but Jini wasn't taught anything. She was musically ignored, but she taught herself anyway, by ear. She picked out tunes on the mandolin, but still her parents saw only the potential of a doctor in the family and sent her to the science stream at school. In 1947, as India was partitioned, her father felt it would be safer for pro-British Parsees to be in England, so the whole family moved to London. A dank London, yet to be rebuilt after the war, rationing still in place with one egg a week, an ounce of butter a week, one bottle of milk, but a special ration for foreigners so they could buy sweets.

Jini's siblings couldn't stand England, and begged their father to return to balmy, rich Bombay. Jini refused to leave.

'I am going to learn the violin.'

At seventeen this young Indian woman was left alone in London, applying for places at music colleges. None would take her, perhaps unsurprisingly, as Jini couldn't play anything, apart from the mandolin by ear. To study the violin, you needed to be able to play it.

One day Jini was waiting for a train at Waterloo Station. She saw a lady with a violin, and sidled up to her on her bench.

'Are you a violin teacher?'

'No, I am studying the violin.'

'In the school or college?'

'No, privately.'

The violinist gave Jini the address of her teacher, a lady called Gladys Noon. Gladys Noon changed Jini's life. Well, Jini changed her own life, but Gladys Noon invited Jini to stay with her, taught her, encouraged her, and after two and a half years Jini gained distinction in her grade eight. She could go to college after all.

And then Jini's parents wrote to her from Bombay and told her to return. She had done what she wanted for long enough. They had a nice young man lined up for her to marry.

Jini went back to Bombay.

Once again somebody stepped in to help her. Her brother-in-law saw how distressed Jini was and suggested she be allowed to return to England, so that her talent was not wasted. Jini's father relented and she returned to London, again to the care of Gladys Noon. Jini began to have lessons with Max Rostal, probably the most famous violin teacher in London at that time. The Amadeus Quartet had studied with him, as had Eli Goren. My own musical heritage is enormously influenced by his teaching. He had studied with Carl Flesch, who had studied with Jakob Grün, who had studied with Joseph Böhm, who had worked with Beethoven. Max Rostal was at the heart of music-making in England. But he wasn't for Jini.

She reeled from his singular approach to technique and quickly chose a different path, studying with the Spanish violinist Antonio Brosa. Brosa was a famous soloist, who performed in Proms concerts many times from 1927 to 1958, including a couple of first nights. He was a friend of Britten, with whom he had worked on the Britten violin concerto. Max Rostal's style didn't suit Jini, but Brosa's did. Brosa even played on a violin connected with India, the Viceroy Strad. He was enormously generous with his time, teaching Jini every Friday afternoon for four hours (lessons are usually an hour), and only charging half his rate of five guineas a lesson. Now Jini was flying with her violin, learning concertos, sonatas, soaking in as much as she could, to be able to pass this priceless knowledge on to musicians in India. Jini studied with Brosa for three years.

She eventually returned to Mumbai in the sixties and began to teach, to share the value of the musical jewels she had taken charge of. She began with a four-and-a-half-year-old violin student, and ended up with a whole chamber orchestra.

The difficulty of Jini's work, always struggling against prejudice, ignorance and bureaucracy, is hard to comprehend. To do this for a few months, a year or so, is perhaps imaginable, but

Jini has been building the Bombay Chamber Orchestra for fifty years. Through the Indian Emergency, through famines, through financial crises, through assassinations of leaders, through the interminable, occasionally corrupt and always frustrating Indian bureaucratic maze.

At one point in our interview, after Jini's manservant had brought up pomegranate juice for me, Jini went to a dusty corner behind her grand piano and dug out a creased envelope. She pulled out a document half her size, a certificate for an MBE, awarded for services to music. Jini has brought a great big branch of the classical music tree to tens of thousands of Indians. Her legacy is simply phenomenal.

The gala concert was given at the National Centre for Performing Arts, on the same day the death was reported of Pandit Ravi Shankar.

The foyer to the concert hall includes a marble staircase and chandelier, donated by a Parsee family. The hall was packed — women in silk saris with the most elegant of rustles as they passed, keen, thin young students, stately government officials, and twenty of the slum children whose performance had originally inspired me to come to India. The orchestra, conducted by the Englishman Patrick Bailey, played as if they were playing for the whole of the country. After Rimsky-Korsakov, Rachmaninov and Bizet, we played the *Knightsbridge March* by Eric Coates as an encore. Something about the Victorian-ness of this piece was perfectly apt for such a setting.

Many of my new friends had come from afar, from Goa, from Sri Lanka, to play together in the orchestra; there was a real feeling of appreciation in what we were doing, what was available at our fingertips. Although there were some out-of-tune bits and and some squeaky bits, the way we all played together as a team meant we pulled each other through. There was no meanness among the players, no judgement, merely a wonder at how lucky we were to have this opportunity. The whole of the Bombay Chamber Orchestra was truly greater than the sum of its parts. This concert, I am certain, will remain one of the most moving I have ever taken part in.

Besides loving playing the viola again, I revelled in the lack of pressure of this day, the simple appreciation of the music, the audience, the sheer privilege and good fortune of being able to play a musical instrument with other people. The deepest communication of all.

B flat major/minor

Two flats for B flat major are left, E and B. B flat minor, has five flats. B flat major is a gloriously resonant key for brass and winds and is the key to the opening of the *Star Wars* theme. Is there anything more thrilling than that opening chord?

B flat minor in my mind is the darkest of the minor keys, a matt black key. B flat minor is a key to illustrate somebody trapped underground, with no escape …

I had decided to take a side trip from Pakistan into India. I cycled to Amritsar from Lahore in just a few hours, but from Amritsar I was happy to take a train to Delhi and on to Mumbai. I was planning to meet a Dutch friend there, from where we would cycle down the coast then up into the hill stations around Pune. I had to get Vita and myself to Mumbai first, which was not going to be easy.

Travelling by bicycle is relatively simple. You pump up your tyres, you oil your chain, you hop on, and off you go. Travelling with a bicycle on Indian trains is the complete opposite; in fact it is probably about the most problematic public transport challenge in the world. It should really be included in one of those race-around-the-world programmes — 'Take an expensive-looking, exotic foreign bicycle that people will want to ride away with; book it, your luggage and yourself onto two trains with only a short time to get across New Delhi to the next railway station. No maps will be provided.'

I quickly realised that if you need to book something into the luggage car at an Indian railway station, it is worth the money to hire a porter. I had succeeded in booking a third-class ticket from Amritsar to Delhi, then a sleeper on the overnight train from Delhi to Mumbai. This was an effort in itself, as I stood in the women's queue and people shot me filthy 'you are not a woman' glances. I turned up at the station the next morning with Vita and was accosted by a fierce crowd of porters, all wanting to help me. I chose the one with the kindest face, gave him my luggage and we made our way to the end of the platform where the luggage car would stop. I filled in forms in triplicate, which are probably still in a ledger somewhere in Indian Railway land, and waited.

The train was late. This was bad. I had three hours to get across Delhi, I only had a compass and a topographical map to guide me, and I really didn't want to miss that sleeper train. Finally, after an hour, the first train shambled in and we all shoved ourselves into our prescribed spaces.

The journey was truly beautiful, the white Indian light strewing itself across the wheat fields. The light was already so intense; all but the brightest of colours had evaporated. I watched a Sikh man dress his head with his turban, his friend holding the metres of material out as the Sikh's hands turned it one way and then the other around his head. Since the man opposite me was sticking his feet into my thighs, I ended up standing in the open doorway of the train, the thick, woolly air buffeting my face. Coming from Pakistan, where people were so respectful and it is considered the height of rudeness to show somebody the soles of your feet, I was truly shocked. Then I was shocked at how shocked I was. That crowd of Pakistan stayed with me for a long time. I think they are still there.

The train arrived in New Delhi an hour and a half late. So I had an hour and a half to have my luggage form stamped by the Delhi inspector, collect Vita, get across Delhi and find the next station. There was no chance of making that next train, but I was going to give it my best shot.

The Delhi inspector had clearly tired of sitting at a desk in an office so had brought his desk to the platform. This was good, as it made it easy to find him (on platform two), but bad, as it made it easier for him to ignore me. As politely as I could, I showed him my form and asked him to give it his stamp of approval. Somewhere, in one of those desk drawers was the stamp. The key to me getting the next train.

The inspector didn't meet my eyes. Bad sign. He shrugged his shoulders, sat down importantly and proceeded to shuffle around dozens of tatty forms, just like mine, on his desk.

'Stay calm, stay polite.' My mantra for travel, if not life.

It didn't help.

The fat inspector, singlet stained brown under his arms, sat purposefully at his desk. I stood a little behind him, trying to balance the desire to remind him of my presence and the URGENT NEED TO GET MY FORM STAMPED, with being polite and not hassling him.

It didn't help.

The fat inspector put down the forms he was glacially reorganising and then bent over to his left, pulled some keys from his trouser pocket and unlocked the bottom drawer.

'This is it, the stamp is in that drawer, of course it is, what else could be under lock and key?'

His lunch.

Endless minutes I stood there watching him eat aloo paratha, absolutely forbidding myself to say anything, as it would only mean I would be there until dinnertime. I began to see the rest of my life spent waiting on this platform in Delhi, growing old as the fat inspector grew fatter.

Thank heavens it wasn't a multi-course thali his wife had given him. His bite was big, the paratha disappeared in about five mouthfuls and, after some swipes with a greasy cloth around his chops, he opened the same drawer, the precious lunch drawer, and took out a stamp. By now I didn't allow myself any hope. I merely wondered what this might be a stamp for; maybe one for his wife, confirming that lunch had been eaten.

The fat inspector turned around, still avoiding looking at

me, beckoned for my form, and stamped it. I now had less than an hour to get across Delhi to the next station.

Vita is a very attractive bike with a rather unusual frame, and I was desperately worried somebody would spot her and race her off into the chemically enhanced sunset, while I dillied and dallied at the other end of the platform. I ran as hard as my cyclist's legs would let me down to the luggage car and there she stood, leaning casually against a pillar, waiting for me. If she had eyebrows, one of them would have been nonchalantly raised.

Right, what was I going to do? One solitary option: get a rickshaw.

Glance around you now, where you are sitting/standing/lying; look about a metre to the side of you, and half a metre in front. That is about the size of the sitting area in a rickshaw. Vita and I are bigger. A lot bigger.

I ran out to the rickshaw area and spoke to the first rickshaw off the rank.

'Hello, can you take me to Hazrat Nizamuddin Station, please?'

The driver looked completely overwhelmed, as if I had asked him to transport a hippopotamus to Africa. He shook his head. I reckoned it was going to be easier to try a few drivers first, rather than waste precious time trying to persuade a single one. I went down the line.

No.

No.

No.

What?

Yes. Aha.

At a ridiculous price, probably a week's wages, but he was going to earn it. I took the panniers off Vita, eased her back wheel into the corner of the rickshaw, turned her handlebars to try and reduce rickshaw overflow, and we headed out in to the Delhi traffic.

The joy of seeing the Gate of India fly past, with Vita of the Overflow spinning her front wheel in thin air, was worth every rupee. We arrived at the station with twenty minutes to spare.

Vita looked a little disconcerted and awry as I pulled her from the rickshaw, like a distinguished lady who has had to go on a donkey ride. We pushed our way through the crowds, found a red-shirted porter to help find my carriage and Vita's, and waited on the platform for the train to Mumbai. The sun was beginning to set.

Some pieces of music can feel like a race: Mozart final movements of pretty much anything, Beethoven scherzos, anything in six eight time, and Bach's Brandenburg Concerto No. 6.

The reason Bach wrote these Brandenburg concertos is because he went shopping. Not for vegetables, but for a harpsichord.

Poor old J.S. Such endless work, endless children, untalented employers and frustrating students. Bach never seemed to be particularly happy in his work situation. He was imprisoned for a month by the Duke in Weimar for wanting to leave his employment, but straight away got another gig with the Prince in Anhalt-Cöthen. This new employer was Calvinist, so he didn't need any fancy music for religious services; this freed up a lot of Bach's time and meant that he could devote more attention to secular music, written for the brilliant players at the court. His relationship with the prince was excellent, until a new prince's wife came along. She was not so keen on music, the prince became less interested in playing the viola da gamba and therefore having Bach write for him, so Bach began to look around for a new gig. He wasn't going to stay somewhere he wasn't appreciated.

Bach had to go to Berlin to buy a new harpsichord, and while he was there he met the Margrave of Brandenburg in the harpsichord shop. Bach promised to send the Margrave some compositions, thinking he might get a job out of it.

Instead of a one-page CV from J.S. Bach, the Margrave received six concertos, six of the greatest pieces ever composed. And probably the greatest CV in history. The Margrave's orchestra never played them, since his musicians weren't up to the task, and the manuscripts were left undiscovered in his library for nearly a hundred years.

It is hard to imagine life now without this music, without the joy of these six extremely varied pieces, all highly virtuosic, and with the final one devoted to the viola.

Since the Prince in Cöthen played the viola da gamba, Bach included it in the final concerto in B flat major. It is scored for two violas da bracchio (of the arm), two violas da gamba (of the leg), a cello, a violone (a large viol) and harpsichord. Note the absence of violins (hurrah).

Because there are no high instruments, the sound of the piece is comforting and chocolatey; it isn't at all sleepy, it's just not strident. This is music to play after a superb meal, when you are relaxed and don't need to prove anything. It's nimble older-person music.

It is tricky though. I showed this to my viola teacher Mr Stace when I was about fifteen, and he advised me to wait a year or so. I didn't, of course, and played it with my mate Julia, busking in short, cold English summers. At best we would make about twenty quid, ten of those donated by Gran'ma.

The two violas are the stars of the show. They race around each other in close canon, or imitation, playing chasey among the semiquavers. They woo each other for a while, but then it disintegrates with a quick slap and the chase is on again, in another place, another key. One of the great delights for me, as a viola player, is how much fun this piece is to play. Even the slow movement is not that mournful, as so much viola music can be. The final movement is in galloping six eight, a guarantee for a good time. Bach, with this music, puts the viola in a gleeful, almost virtuosic place, somewhere we are not usually at home.

This piece is Alex's favourite in *A Clockwork Orange*. At least the guy had good taste in something. And it's fun to have running through your head when you are racing across Delhi in a rickshaw.

The sleeper train pulled into the station in Delhi, right on time. Just before it blocked my view, I noticed a group of workmen in dhotis cross the tracks at the end of their day's work.

My porter took me down to the luggage car and I tucked Vita into her berth between bulging cardboard boxes. We headed back up the train to find my carriage and, as we did, a crowd of passengers began to grow in the middle of the platform, all looking underneath the train at something on the tracks.

You know that human behaviour, of not being able to stop yourself looking where other people are looking? As I got closer, my eyes turned to underneath the carriage. There to the left, lying on the gravel, was one of the workmen. His right leg had been severed by the train.

It took a moment to realise what I was seeing. I remember so clearly his astonished face, the darkness of his leg, the white of his fat and the silence of the crowd. Then, compelled as before, I followed the crowd's gaze to the right. There, in front of me, was the rest of his leg in two pieces. The mid-section, the knee perfectly intact, and the ankle and foot, left standing on the white stones. Ready to hold up a body.

Medics rushed under the train, pulled him out and ran off with him on a stretcher. The two sections of leg were left on the tracks. I asked a man standing next to me if he thought the workman would survive. He shrugged his shoulders. This was India. Everybody survives, if that is their fate.

B flat minor.

Erase every colour, stop all the clocks, close the books, silence the songs. B flat minor is the key of nothing.

Shostakovich wrote fifteen quartets. The first is a jaunty little work, the mood relatively upbeat; the third is full of love and disappointment; with the eighth quartet, written after a visit to Dresden in 1960, he wounds us all, yet despite the depictions of bombings and aircraft drones even this work ends in a major key. His thirteenth, though, depicts the horror of life in a way that is unrelenting from beginning to end. In our life, the police often protect us from knowledge of the most horrific crimes, but in this B flat minor work Shostakovich offers us no protection. If you are going to listen to this piece, make sure you have a friend to call afterwards. Seriously.

After my student quartet had learnt Webern, Dr Chris Rowland gave us Mendelssohn; then, for our final piece at the Royal Northern, Shostakovich 13. Chris' quartet, the Fitzwilliam, had premiered No. 13 in England, and some of the quartet had met Shostakovich and discussed the interpretation of it with him. So when we learnt this from Chris, we were virtually learning it from Shostakovich.

Where Bach's Sixth Brandenburg Concerto is free and frivolous, this quartet, heavily featuring the viola, is the opposite. Even the tempo is constrained — adagio; double speed; adagio. The piece is written in one dreadful movement. Listening to and playing this piece dozens of times, I can find no moment of joy, no moment of exhilaration, no relaxation, no optimism.

The quartet was dedicated to Vadim Vasilyevich Borisovsky, the violist of the Beethoven Quartet. Throughout the piece, the sadness of the viola leads the way to a country of desolation for the others. Although the piece is in B flat minor, a series of notes seemingly without key begin the music, played by the viola alone. This is a tone row, the system of composing developed by Schoenberg and rarely used to such great effect as here. Although each of the twelve semitones in the octave is used, there is still a real sense of key, of the world of B flat minor. Shostakovich uses these twelve different sounds so brilliantly that it is only when you hear it a few times you realise that it is in fact a tone row. There is such an overwhelming intent to the phrase that the tone row becomes the perfect musical vehicle. Eventually the other three join the viola, which is now in a place that, after only a few bars, is undoubtedly hell.

But it is a hell on earth. It is a hell full of small-minded, picky, tight-mouthed people, people who decide matters of life and death and art; a hell of the violins as they pick out mean, starved sounds from their instruments while the others around them mock and sneer; a hell of music for all the ugly-souled, unthinking, self-serving people in the world, of whom too many had power over Shostakovich. This hell never ended for him, neither in his life nor in this piece; it just kept on getting worse.

Shostakovich had terrible health (like so many composers — Mozart, Beethoven, Tchaikovsky, Chopin, Schubert, Schumann) and towards the end of his life suffered heart attacks, and falls in which he broke both his legs. Shostakovich wrote this quartet between spells in orthopaedic clinics, for treatment for his broken legs. Shostakovich smoked without end and drank vodka, possibly contributing to the falls. Oh, and the heart attacks.

But wouldn't you drink and smoke if you were in his shoes? The pressure of the Communist Party on his private and public life since the 1920s, the denunciations, the humiliations, the deaths and murders of his closest friends, the perpetual balancing act of keeping his integrity as an artist and keeping the apparatchiks happy. Perhaps we should wonder at how amazingly long Shostakovich *did* live in such circumstances.

As the sneering music comes to a climax, the three-quaver motif repeated throughout this part is played with ferocity and true spite, a stab not just to your heart, but also to your spirit. And again the viola emerges as a leader, taking you deeper and deeper into the darkness.

The three quavers turn into pizzicato combined with a fierce viola trill, leading into the middle section. It is here that a jolt explodes from the quartet, a jolt that makes you feel sick with anxiety.

Shostakovich directs that the four musicians hit their instruments with the ends of their bows. It sounds like a knock from another world, a knock from somebody who knows they can't come back, but who wants you to know that, at some point, their misery will be yours too.

When my quartet performed this, we used a fifth instrument, actually the violin I had learnt on as an eight-year-old. We placed it in the middle of the music stands, bridge down, and whacked the back of it. The visual drama of this, an instrument first of all being placed *face down,* then being hit, shocked the audience. It was like watching somebody being caned. You could feel that people were sickened by it. What made it worse was that the hits seemed random, entirely unpredictable within the rhythm of the piece, so each one was a whole new shock.

As the double speed section gives way to the opening speed again, the viola returns with the opening tone row. The others join in with the same lament as before, this time leading to a cello outburst that seems to change the mood, to make it meeker. The violin pulls the music up into the sky and only then is there a single chord of rest. E major, the key of sunshine.

From here an excruciating intertwining of cello and viola takes us further and further into the hopelessness, made even worse after that one flicker of light. And when the two violins enter with their plaint, you know the deal is done. The door is shut. The viola is left alone in a padded cell, only the knock as a reminder that anybody was ever your friend, ever your lover, ever your trustee. The music drifts up, higher than any other viola part in the repertoire. It reaches a top top A, then, the last weary note, a B flat. It starts quietly, the two violins joining on the same vertiginous pitch, and in a flash of crescendo, life ends.

The final time my quartet played this at college, a man sat in the front row in a wheelchair, his leg muscles atrophied. At the last moment, when it seemed like the air has been sucked out of the room, he leapt from his chair in a spasm.

From the Tibetan area of China, I cycled down through panda forests (I didn't see any) to Suzhou. This was a bit of a way station; I met up with Chris and Shelagh, friends from Hong Kong, ate a lot of very spicy food, talked to an Englishwoman about becoming a chef on a yacht, drank a lot of beer, and relaxed.

I would regret doing that.

By now it was November and I planned my route through Sichuan Province, then onto Guizhou and finally Guangzhou, bordering Hong Kong. I had had my visa extended, so was not particularly stressed about cycling quickly and was looking forward to this final month of the journey. A time to ruminate on what I had seen and learnt, and to enjoy being alone and carefree.

I left Chengdu on a Wednesday. Due to the time difference it was still the first Tuesday in November in the United States, and it was the year George Dubya was going up against Al Gore in the presidential election. I planned a day of cycling a mere one hundred and fifty kilometres (a ride round the block for me by now), with regular stops for election updates on my shortwave radio.

Off I went, out of the huge city of Chengdu, past miles of mono-architecture and, finally, into the Sichuan countryside. Bushes of Sichuan peppers, dried persimmons for sale, truly awful and dangerous driving, but all of it going over my head. The election was turning out to be too close to call. The commentators on the BBC World Service were beside themselves with excitement and I listened to the radio as often as possible. Still, I made it to Neijiang by about four, just as school was out. I freewheeled down a small hill on the outskirts of town, thinking about what would happen to the world if Bush got in. Vita was running beautifully since I had given her a service in Chengdu and was completely silent apart from the whispering Shimano freewheel. Young schoolboys walked down the hill by the road and, suddenly, bang, one of them stepped into my path and the whole weight of myself and Vita, travelling at about thirty kilometres an hour, slammed into his side. He smacked down onto the tarmac as I tried to lessen the impact by braking and falling. It didn't work; the boy was unconscious.

The next moments happened in a complete daze. A huge crowd gathered immediately and the boy was taken to a food shop. People picked me up as well and firmly directed me to the same place. There was no way I was going to be allowed to leave. In my simple Mandarin I apologised profusely and tried to say that the boy had stepped out without looking. I didn't know it at the time, but this subtlety wouldn't have mattered; it was my fault, as I was driving the vehicle. Pedestrians take no responsibility in China.

The police and an ambulance were called, and the boy, now awake and with a nasty graze on his forehead, was whisked off to hospital. I was left sitting in the shop with a tense crowd around me until the police arrived in a van. They put Vita and me into it and took me to the police station.

Fuck. Fuck fuck FUCK.

A police officer sat me down in his office and pulled a government-issue 'How to Speak English for Police' handbook from his desk drawer. A combination of that and my Mandarin allowed us a conversation in which he told me the boy had been taken for a scan at a bigger hospital and that I would have to pay for it. I had just changed a bunch of money in

Chengdu, my final travellers' cheque, so luckily I was cashed up with about $US400. The money wouldn't be a problem for then, but the boy's health and getting more money afterwards would be.

The boy's relatives, an uncle and aunt, came and sat in the office with us. We sat there for six hours, waiting for word from the hospital. I chain-smoked, absolutely stressed out of my mind. What if the boy died? What if he had brain damage? What the fuck was going to happen to me in this tiny town in the middle of China?

You idiot, I shouted at myself. If you had been concentrating and not so concerned with that bloody election, this wouldn't have happened. You absolute bloody arsehole. I was so fucked.

After six hours the father of the boy returned. The boy was all right. The scan had been done and it was over. I handed over nearly all my cash and was allowed to leave.

I wandered out into the night, not sure what to do, where to go, how to get more money. It was about 10pm and I had about fifty yuan left, about a dollar.

The police officer followed me out. He gestured to me to go with him and we walked to a nearby hotel. I didn't have enough money for the foreigners' rate, but he spoke to the manager so that I could pay the cheaper local rate — fifty yuan.

And then he took me out for dinner.

F major/minor

As you can probably imagine, it took a while to recover from the shock of knocking the boy over. The next morning I went to the local bank and tried to get some money out on my credit card, by now having absolutely no money left. The bank couldn't do the transaction, they didn't have the technology, so my only choice was to backtrack to Chengdu. Off I set, one hundred and fifty kilometres with no food and a terrible feeling in my soul. I had been unbelievably lucky, but the worry that the boy would have a relapse stayed with me for the next month until I finally left China. For a long time I felt suspended in a worry-machine, not quite on the ground. My equilibrium had taken a severe beating.

Back in Chengdu, I called my mum (something I had hardly done on the whole trip) and told her what had happened.

And she said exactly what I wanted to hear:
'Well Binx, you're nearly there, keep your chin up!'

F major is the key of the earth, of grounding, of calm. Beethoven used it often, including for his first and his last quartet, for two of his symphonies; Brahms uses it for his third symphony, Haydn uses it for a bunch of quartets, Mozart for sonatas, opera arias, quartets and concertos. Because there is only one remaining flat, B flat, the string instruments are extremely open and the dominant and tonic on the bottom C string of the violas and cellos add a real lustre to the sound. I really love F major, it is the key of homecoming.

Beethoven's Sixth Symphony, the *Pastoral*, is in F major. He wrote it in 1807 and, highly unusual for the times, included a brief description for each movement in its title:

I. Allegro ma non troppo (joyful but not too much) — Awakening of feelings upon arriving in the countryside
II. Andante molto moto (at walking speed with a lot of movement) — Scene at the Creek ('Bach' in German)
III. Allegro (joyful) — Joyful reunion of peasants (woo-hoo)
IV. Allegro — The Tempest
V. Allegretto (joyful-ish) — Feelings of joy and gratitude after the storm

Beethoven, while living in Vienna, wrote to one of his friends that, 'No one can love the country as much as I do.' The Vienna Woods were close by, as was the little town of Heiligenstadt where he wrote his heartbreaking testament in which he admits his growing deafness. To relieve the stress on his dying hearing he spent as much time as possible here, away from the noise and energy of the big city. When Beethoven writes about the awakening of feelings on arrival in the country, you can imagine that this is very much what would have happened to him; finally he could listen to his inner voice, his composing voice.

People often wonder how Beethoven composed without being able to hear for much of his life, but just think of a tune now in your head, without singing it out loud; that is what Beethoven did. The difference perhaps being (I don't want to make any assumptions about your own ability) that he had the power of imaging an entire orchestra inside his head.

The *Pastoral Symphony* opens with a low F in the cellos and an open C in the violas, making an open fifth, like a drone. The violins play a folk melody that quickly gets taken up by the entire orchestra. What strikes me about this piece today, after playing and listening to it countless times, is how carefree it is, and how it seems to be made up of little kernels of melody, repeated over and over again. Just as nature repeats her beauties of trees and leaves and rivers and flowers, so Beethoven takes a single idea and subtly varies it. It really is an ode to nature.

The slow movement makes you want to find a patch of grass and sun and a bottle of beer and a dog and just *be*. And in the fourth movement, when the storm strikes, the world is defiant against the rumbles and batterings of the timpani and, as the hatches are un-battened and we come out again into the open air, that glorious happy chord of the beginning is repeated, this time with a horn call encouraging us to come out from our shelter and make our way home. It is the simplest of music, fifths and octaves. The horn, its home note being F, is the perfect instrument to beckon us in this way. And so we follow the beckoning, and arrive where we started.

At some point I realised that I would not become a professional cellist. It is hard to say when I realised, maybe one morning as I tried to warm up my hand to stretch comfortably on the fingerboard and failed once again, maybe when I was playing in an orchestra and was getting frustrated at not being able to hear myself like I could as a violist, maybe one afternoon when I was playing Bach and it was still out of tune and lumpy. I know when it wasn't — when I played quartets. Other things slowly took over my time — radio, even sitar for a while. I still played the cello, but it was more and more as an amateur, in the true sense of the word.

George Harrison helped me see the way forward. In the documentary *Living in the Material World* George recalls how he moved from guitar to sitar, then back to guitar.

'There are thousands of great sitar players, but only a few who play the guitar like I do.'

Since I had started playing the viola again, so that I could play and teach it in Kabul, what had disintegrated into a threadbare love in Hong Kong was now reborn into a mature, full-blown passion. The viola had become the instrument that I had always thought the cello would be — an expression of my soul.

I accepted for the first time that I am not a cellist, I am a viola player.

Something happens to your heart when you play an instrument you love. The heart seems to slow and quicken at the same time, the thrill and the balm affect you in equal measure. It is similar to being in the presence of someone you love very deeply.

My love for the viola became more profound during my visit to Kabul, but also my love for music. Norbert Brainin had once told my quartet:

'Music is the most important. Never forget, to be a musician is the most important. You nurse peoples' souls.'

Until I travelled to Kabul, played viola with the students there and saw how much music meant to them, I had not fully understood Professor Brainin's entreaty. Music, in its invisibility, is the greatest force in the world.

Music is love.

I started out again from Chengdu, going a different way this time to avoid Neijiang. On an intensely foggy October morning I crossed the Yangtze at Chongqing and headed into some of the poorest parts of China, places where people were still ploughing with buffalo and living in shacks. The road wound up through steep mountains in Guizhou Province; the surfaces were crumbling and the people tired and reserved. I was still reading *War and Peace* at this point, and as the French soldiers tramped through freezing mud in Russia, I did the same in China. In one place a stretch of road about fifty kilometres long had been completely dug up, leaving mud half a wheel height high; my only option was to grab a lift on a truck. Three young Chinese people took Vita to the back of the truck and I hopped up into the cab. After a few minutes of nodding and greetings, one of the men did something eminently surprising — with his thumb, he pressed hard on the bony bridge of my nose.

'Wow!' he exclaimed.

What could I do? I pressed his squishy non-bony bridge in return.

Although I had managed to get more money out on a card, I had to be a little careful and try to stay in the cheapest of hostels. I had a budget to keep to and was doing well until I realised a large amount of my money, about half, had gone missing. I searched frantically everywhere and couldn't find it. Then, as I looked at my rain jacket, I saw that the side pocket was open. This was where I had put the money in a rush one morning and it must have fallen out. All I could hope was that somebody who really needed that money had found it. Things were now desperate until my brother came and met me in Guilin; I eked out my food and stopped eating dinner.

There was one final hope: my belt was also a money belt and months ago I had put a $US100 bill in there as a last resort. I went along to a bank, proudly presented the bill to exchange it and the clerk examined it slowly. She shook her head. They wouldn't take the bill because my sweat had soaked through the leather belt and stained the money.

I lost a lot of weight.

Closer and closer. The map seemed to shrink to a tiny bit of China, the only bit I now cared about. As I approached Hong Kong, now with my big brother beside me cycling through a classical Chinese painting of the limestone mountains of Guilin, my map became useless since the area had changed so rapidly. There didn't seem to be any map that was up to date. My days were now punctuated by continual stops at confusing junctions, asking people the way to the next town. If they knew they drew me a little map, but often they didn't know and pointed me in the wrong direction. Perhaps their world was so limited they didn't need to know, or perhaps they were so lost themselves in this polluted, horrific, cramped place they just couldn't tell me. I had cycled across deserts and plateaus and continental watersheds and grasslands, yet the final days were spent cycling through a miserable vision of humanity's future. Somehow, with a series of tiny hand-drawn maps from local people, I made it to the border with Hong Kong at Shenzhen.

When I had lived in Hong Kong I had come over the border a few times, back before the Handover in 1997. The thrill of being in mainland China had tempted me, but this area was a special economic zone and it wasn't like the rest of China at all. It was closer to Hong Kong, sort of a copy Hong Kong back then, and now it was becoming an über Hong Kong, with glamorous hotels, apartment blocks and malls shooting up. There hadn't been any buffalo ploughing here for a long time.

* * *

When I was studying at the Royal Academy in London, I cycled through Regent's Park every day. Around the rose bushes, past the bandstand, along the lake and finally onto Marylebone Road and the academy. Every day I watched the gardeners in their blue boiler suits working outside creating beauty, as I made my way to my inside world of being a musician. When our quartet split up, I decided to take some time off being a musician and went to the park's office to ask for a job as a gardener. Remarkably, Bob the head gardener agreed to employ me, with the strict condition that I return to music at the end of the summer.

I worked in the park for three months, mostly weeding and eventually being given the great honour of pruning the roses. I loved it, it gave me a completely different challenge at a time when music had lost its joy to me and I was losing my way. I found my musical way again, left the garden and eventually got a job with Yehudi Menuhin's English String Orchestra. If I hadn't taken that time and instead had simply forced my way through, I may well have given up music for good.

After a few months of gardening I started practising the viola again, with one of my favourite pieces, the F minor Sonata by Brahms. The sonata is one of the two he wrote for the clarinet; this one has much more drama, especially in the first movement. It is marked allegro appassionato and is simply furious and unrelenting. F minor on the viola is a magnificent key. You find yourself playing high up on the C string to keep the melodies smooth, and the key sits well under your left hand as well. The richness of the viola comes to the fore, but not so much that it is overwhelming, as can be the case in C or G minor. F minor is angry, but it is graceful, old anger from many generations of disappointment. The middle movements are in the relative major, A flat, but all that lightness is merely an interval before the ferocity of the final movement, which returns to F minor.

When I was in Pakistan and had been so sick in the south, I became a little depressed. I no longer woke with a spring in my step, and I felt the trip was starting to slip away from me. I had begun to count the kilometres to the next town, rather than wondering what would be around the next corner. I decided I would need to break the trip, go back to Europe and see my family and have a rest. I had promised Bob the gardener I would return to the viola, and I did. I made myself the same promise I had made to Bob, that I would return and continue my journey. After two months I did, picking up where I had left off in Lahore, refreshed and enjoying it again. If I hadn't taken that time, I don't think I would have finished the trip or, worse, I would have finished the trip in the wrong spirit.

The final morning.

I had saved a special cycling jersey for this day, the king of the mountains polka dot jersey from the Tour de France. It was pristine, red and white, in its vacuum bag. I chose my favourite black knicks (a huge choice of them or the blue ones), put on the jersey, pumped up Vita's tyres, packed for the last time and headed towards the Immigration building and Hong Kong.

One of the reasons for doing this trip was to raise money for a school in Hong Kong for kids with special needs. My friend Terry's son Simon went to this school and the money people donated paid for a year's music therapy for the kids. Terry had a friend in the police so they had arranged to meet me at Immigration, then I would ride from the border through the normally off-limits area for cyclists.

At the appointed time, after clearing Customs in China and breathing a huge sigh of relief that the boy I had knocked over hadn't died and that I wouldn't be arrested at the last minute, I crossed the border to my final country, to Hong Kong. The police officer took me to a private room to be stamped in and then Vita and I were taken to a waiting police motorbike escort. Vita had had a special wash, as had I, and it was a perfect warm day, 9 December 2000. Nothing could disturb my happiness.

Although I was now in Hong Kong, there was still quite a way to go to my final stop at the bottom of Hong Kong Island and the fishing village of Shek O. About eighty kilometres. I left the border area, waved goodbye to my police escort and took great delight cycling along the same bikeway where Chris the American and I had had the original journey idea all those lifetimes ago. As I went over the hills from the New Territories into the Kowloon Peninsula, the extreme intensity of Hong Kong hit me.

With motorbikes and trucks and taxis surrounding me as I made my way down Nathan Road, I told myself, 'Don't screw up now, Ayresie.' The thought of another accident shadowed me then and it does still.

There was a reception planned for me at the Kowloon Hotel with my friends and some press; then I had been given more special permission to catch the underground train, the MTR, under the harbour. From there I would cycle over the island to Shek O.

I forgot which way to enter the one-way street where the hotel is and I ended up arriving behind my friends as they all looked the wrong way, waiting for me. After all those months, I had forgotten what a hug felt like. The happiness on my friends' faces, that I had managed to finish this ride, was incredibly moving. We went inside to eat cakes decorated with cyclists and be interviewed by the press and start the long road of assimilation back into society.

More police escorted me via the train to the island and I began my last ever section of the ride. As I had dragged my wheels, reluctant to leave Pakistan, I dragged my wheels here, so reluctant to stop. If I stopped moving, would I fall over? In those last kilometres I considered carrying on, cycling to Australia, or round the world.

And then, the ultimate descent into Shek O. I had dreamt about this descent, I had fantasised about it and, when I needed succour, I had cycled it dozens of times in my head. Now, as Vita's wheels accelerated and I rode the last few bends to the home straight and the beach, tears streamed down my cheeks, to be lifted away in the wind. And then the final cycle, through a crowd of friends, kids and parents from the special needs school, the policeman from the border, Terry and Simon, all there to celebrate sixteen thousand kilometres of cycling, hundreds of nights alone, thousands of people met, hundreds of roadside concerts, many borders negotiated, difficult choices made, dangers gone through, loneliness accepted, a life-changing desire fulfilled.

I phoned both my parents and told them I had finished what I had set out to do. They both, separately, said something they had never before said to me:

'Binx, I'm proud of you.'

C major/minor

Here we are, back at the beginning. The flats have gone and the sharps are yet to come. It is a moment of stillness, before the journey begins again.

When people embark on huge journeys of any sort, physical or academic or spiritual, it seems that the hard work increases when that journey is done.

The road back to real life would turn out to be longer than the one I had been on. After spending so long essentially on my own, simply being with people was hard for me initially. I needed a lot of time alone, I needed to be quiet and I became withdrawn if I didn't have that time. I had spent nearly every day for the last year almost entirely outside, and suddenly I was inside most of the time. The air was too close, people were too close; I had to give myself a serious talking-to, to calm down and relax back into the regular world. I had to get used to the ubiquity of mobile phones and people saying 'Twenty-four seven'. It took me about two years to fully regain my equilibrium.

Luckily I was given a new journey almost straight away.

I began to look for work in Hong Kong and, on the first day of searching, was offered some hours at Radio Television Hong Kong Radio Four, producing and presenting a little bit of arts news twice a week.

As soon as I stepped into the radio studio, it felt like a homecoming. I loved radio from the very first minute, and my love for it continues to grow and deepen. As I worked on different shows and made different types of programmes, the feel of the cadence in my speech became familiar and I developed a way of using it, as I would do music as a musician.

Cadence in music, cadence in cycling, cadence in speech. The three connect more and more as time goes on.

I eventually emigrated from Hong Kong to Australia. After a year of dishwashing in cafés in St Kilda, I was given a little work at the Australian Broadcasting Corporation, on ABC Classic FM. I had had to be very patient. The manager, after hearing my audition tape, said he thought my voice was too English for the audience. Gil Harman, a senior producer, insisted on giving me a chance and, apart from a few doubts about my pronunciation of 'one', things haven't gone too badly since.

Radio is the most intimate of media. As a musician you take people into your care for the time that a piece lasts and I believe that as a radio presenter you have to do the same thing. Presenting classical music, especially early in the morning, means that people listening to your music are vulnerable and raw; it is my beautiful and extremely rewarding job to take their hand and care for their feelings and their memories. I am rewarded a thousandfold. And the openness of the listeners is a continuously inspiring relationship that frequently moves me to tears.

I fell in love with Australia. I fall in love with her still. She has given me better friends than I had ever dreamt of, an optimistic light that illuminates every day, a career that gives more satisfaction than I have ever experienced, and a sense of belonging in a community of great souls. And the love of my life was born in Melbourne and grew up in Bendigo.

Australia is my home.

Just the other week, my quartet had a chance to play in the main hall at the Melbourne Recital Centre. There was a professional chamber music competition going on and the organisers, Chamber Music Australia, had given amateur groups an afternoon to play in the Dame Elisabeth Murdoch Hall, acoustically one of the best in the world. Brenton, Miranda, Martin and I played Mozart's Quartet in C Major, 'The Dissonance' (and yes it was a little).

We rehearsed for a week beforehand, obviously making sure we were well fed and wined before we started playing (well, it *is* important). The rehearsals were too few, but we remained positive and decided that if we totally stuffed up and had to stop in our performance, that really didn't matter. What mattered was the taking part, the making of music. Our journey that week, in the years before as an ensemble and in the years before that as individual musicians, had brought us to this event. We trusted it would be all right and it was. We were brilliant, in our slightly out-of-tune, out-of-time way.

Why did I do my bicycle trip? During that week, a difficult week of quartet rehearsals, live radio broadcasts, interviews, writing this book, giving the concert in the Recital Centre and doing my own practice, the answer arrived every day. Since I finished the trip, indeed for the last thirteen years, the answer has arrived in virtually everything I do.

I made that trip because somewhere deep inside me I knew that life is here to be thrilled by, not to be weighed down by. That by testing ourselves we will slow things down to a speed that we can manage and it will make things simpler; we will distil life to its essential ingredients. Adversity, in enormous and small doses, keeps us alive. Adversity makes us decide what is important and reveals our true selves. And it is by cycling and by playing an instrument that I dare to say I might begin to know myself.

Music saved me. It gave me a constant when much around me was bewildering and often violent. I think it was Sting, the pop musician, who said that being a musician saved him from a life of crime and wastefulness. Music opened a secret door to a shelter where people listened and were kind.

To share the value of music is the resolve of my life.

My childhood was hard. It wasn't as awful as many people's, but it was a big challenge at the time. We four siblings tried to survive it and, in our own very different ways, we did.

Penny eventually changed her behaviour and now works with young offenders, teaching them life skills. She is a superb chef with her own company and has brought up three children, mostly on her own.

Tim became an internationally acclaimed artist, whose art is owned by museums around the world.

Liz's eczema cleared and now she works with drug addicts, making sure they have access to health education. She has been with her partner Polly for over thirty years and they have three sons together.

Gran'ma lived happily until ninety-three, and, thanks to Penny, only moved to a care home in her final few months.

And my mum? It is very hard to say. There were some years latterly when she seemed happier than in my youth, but then she would descend into depression again. She remains in love/hate with my father and will probably do so until the day she dies. Her love for my father destroyed her and it keeps her alive. She is the most remarkable person I know. Mum listens to music every day on the radio and I often think of her when I play my viola.

I rediscovered my true voice by writing this book. I returned to playing the viola when I went to Kabul to teach, and my viola sits over there on the table, waiting for me to start practising it tomorrow.

* * *

When I was eight years old, my mother asked me the most important question of my life.

'Emma, what instrument do you want to play?'

A simple question: what sound do you like? What do your friends play? Who is your favourite music teacher at school? Do you, in fact, particularly care what instrument you play? Or will it simply be a way of passing the time until you find something else to distract you?

Or a question of great depth and difficulty, one that you may not ever be able to answer, a koan; you may as well ask, what language would you like to speak for the rest of your life? What type of people will your friends be? What will evolve to be your fundamental philosophical tenets? Who, indeed, do you want to *be* in this world?

Seeing as I was only eight, I thought the question was the former. I see now, at forty-six and a bit, that it was really the latter.

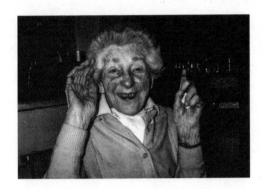

In memory of Tressie Doreen Thompson

Gran'ma

1909–2002

With thanks

Thank you to my mother for your extraordinary ability as a parent. You made us all strong, and for that I will be forever grateful.

Thank you to everyone at ABC Books and HarperCollins, especially Mary Rennie for pulling everything together.

Thank you to Betty, Karla, Paul, Richard and Dr Crock for reading my first draft and being so encouraging.

Thank you to Amanda (Smith), Amanda (Smoth), Hilary and Bob for your endless warmth and love and desserts.

Thank you to Liz and Martin for keeping me well, to Lee and Andrew, my first Australian friends, for introducing me to Arthur Streeton and the idea of beer as a traveller, to Sam for keeping me fit (feel this bicep!), and to Berin for welcoming me back to Aikido.

Thank you to Helen Sharwood, Madame Lash, for helping me to bid 7NT with some confidence.

Thank you to Elizabeth and Don Allen. You created the best thing in the world – a happy family. Thank you for inviting me into it.

Thank you to Nick and Justine for being my bizarrely young mum and dad in Australia. John and Jim want you as their parents too . . .

Thank you to Zac, Phoebe and Lizzie, my first quartet in Australia. You are splendid friends.

Thank you to all the people at the Vipassana Centre in Blackheath, New South Wales. Your compassion and calmness helped me immeasurably.

Thank you to my teachers and to the musicians with whom I have made music over these years.

Thank you to the people I met on my travels. Your hospitality is a life's lesson in generosity of spirit.

Thank you to Brenton, Miranda and Martin, my quartet. Let's keep playing 'The Dissonance'!

Thank you to the listeners to ABC Classic FM. You made me feel truly welcome in Australia.

And finally, thank you to Jane. How are you fixed for the next seventy-five years?

ABC Classics presents a companion album of
works from *Cadence*, compiled by Emma Ayres.
From intimate Bach to grandiloquent Elgar, experience
a vivid journey through the keys and share the music
which has accompanied Emma on her travels.

Available from ABC Shops, ABC Centres,
good music stores and online at
www.abcshop.com.au

ABC
Classics